Spirit

Hearing What's Good, Living What's Good

Milton Howard, Jr.

Spirit

Table of Contents

Deciding To Be On Top 1

I Die Daily - The Practice of Death	2
Putting Empty Feelings to Death	3
Mind Make-Up	5
The Concept of Sorrow	10
The Legacy of Sorrow	15
Limiting Belief #1	12
Limiting Belief #2	15
Fossilization	20

Growing From Small To Big 25

Religious Ideas Versus the Mind	27
The "You" Outside of "You"	29
Growth and Growing	39
What's In the Mirror	45
Removing Fear and Shame	47
Fields of Substance	49
Limiting Belief #3	27
Limiting Belief #4	31
Limiting Belied #5	39
Limiting Belief #6	41

Money, Money, Money - The Spirit of Life 51

The Importance of Things	60
Know Who You Are	66
True Money Patterns	74

The Work of God's Spirit   88

Limiting Belief #7   52
Limiting Belied #8   82

The Sound of God..91

Our True Residence   98
The Sound That Outpaces Problems   99
What's God's Name   101

Limiting Belief #9   94

The Anatomy of Worship...105

The 12 Points of Significance   114
The Misunderstood Kingdom   121
12 Foundations of Success   127
Decision Strategies   141
10 Stages of Decision Making   142

Limiting Belief #10   118

And the Gift of God Is   139

Deciding To Be On Top

Life is incredible, and life remains incredible whether you decide to participate in life or not. The good life never dissipates from your presence, but your mind can mask out the good that's available to you at all times. For various reasons many people have decided to live outside of the life that they want, but this is not life's fault. It's always a choice.

Life does not care what you think. It can't. You are either living a good life or living outside of life. What many people experience now is not actually life. Yes, you are alive, but being "alive" does not mean that you are participating in life. An extreme number of people don't even know what life is and have lost all sensibility towards the true, rewarding, and satisfying existence called life. True life is about capability. Life is about mastering and commanding the things that you want. Are you living your capability?

There are some people who seem to have the Midas touch. Whatever they put their hands to turns out right. They want what they want and then they get it. These are the people who can imagine something and then they can make it happen. Their life is never accidental. They make a decision and then you see what they have decided on unfold in front of them. They live fantastic lives, and they also enjoy the finer things in life. They get things done, but none of this is attributed to religious affiliations or any other belief system. What they do is built within them, and their ability to make a decision comes from a special place. It seems as though they are born with a gift to make things happen. Is this life for everyone or is it just for a privileged few?

I want to begin to immediately help you with this, but I must show you that the people who are ultra-successful in life use the exact same process to gain riches as others who live only to maintain a habit or live a non-productive lifestyle.

What is a non-productive lifestyle? A non-productive lifestyle is any lifestyle that you are not satisfied with, but can't seem to find a way out or a way to make things different. People who are living and are not able to produce what they want in life, have even learned to become religiously comfortable with what's "less".

I Die Daily – The Practice of Death

I'll start here. Both the rich and the poor practice what I call the practice of death. The practice of death is the beginning process of decision-making, but it's done with a different mind or state of consciousness between the social economic classes. Even when it comes to religion and church, most people do not have a clue as to what practicing death is; therefore they don't have the results that they want in their life.

What do I mean by practicing death? Is this some weird book on paranormal spirituality or dark practices? No. It's just the opposite, but you have to be prepared to broaden your understanding in order to get what you want in life. And trust me; you deserve whatever you want in life. Getting what you want in this life is true life, but you can live something other than your true life when you miss some important factors about the reality of how life really works.

Everyone has the same need and this need is to answer a literal chemical set in their body that's associated with the sensation of sorrow. What is sorrow? Sorrow is the calling for "more" when you feel "less". Life will always answer this physiological composition within your body. This composition of sorrow has to be answered with success, because the turning of these inner juices from a dark place to a sense of success gives you a natural high as these chemicals will change forms when you make decisions or accomplish any goal.

Decision-making actuates a physiological alchemy or transition that takes place within every human being, so no decision should ever be made lightly. Some use this process of answering this chemical composition called sorrow to build a great corporation and make millions of dollars by facing their inner sorrow with impeccable decision-making qualities. The key to a satisfied life and a fulfilled life is decision-making. Some use the exact same need to answer this chemical composition called sorrow to smoke a cigarette, eat an extra piece of pie, or stay in an abusive relationship, stay on a dead-end job, and the like.

Note this. Everyone has the need to gain a sense of accomplishment, because accomplishment becomes the answer to this chemical composition called sorrow built within your body, especially when sorrow is accompanied by an empty feeling. What you want to do is put all these empty feelings to death, therefore reaching an end to your current condition or circumstance. But reaching an end is not the answer, nor is it the controlling factor in life. It is the "more" that's wanted once an end is reached that controls all of life. Accomplishment is never fulfilling, because the need for "more" is always present at the point of any accomplishment or reaching a particular goal. "More" is the only true thing that puts "less" to death. So at every point of accomplishment there is always "more" to be gained.

Putting Empty Feelings to Death

This is where accounting becomes vital. At the end of every action that you take there is actually more to be gained or more to do.

The shedding of a negative emotion by replacing it with the sensation of accomplishment is natural. This type of "shedding" is a death. This is what I mean by the practice of death – death is a wearing off of an old sensation and having the ability to gain a new sensation. True success is not about reaching a goal to gain a sensation, but it is about having the ability to grow beyond the wearing off of an old sensation. Some people experience the same sensation over and over again because measurement is not taken after action and they have a hard time breaking out of habits that supply them with the same old experiences time after time.

The ability to grow past an unwanted sensation or feelings stemming from an event or circumstance starts with knowing yourself. Every point of any type of production has to have an image as its starting point in order to know its end, and everything you want to accomplish starts with an image of you. You are the seed to any and everything that you want in life.

If you want something bad enough, an image is created in the mind and then this image is rebuilt into your body physiologically. Once it is built in your body, there is little that can be done to influence the body from a particular direction once it is set within. It is at this time the energy outside of your body is organized to produce and align with the energy of what's in your body. This is the process of Spirit. The chemicals in your body become a powerful system of accomplishment. This is why some people smoke again and again, and some experience success again and again. Both persons practice death by putting the previous existence to death, but some wake up to the same old, same old, and then some wake up to newer and greater things. What's shocking is that both take the same amount of energy whether you are going up or going down.

Note: This is why suicide is so powerful. A person doesn't die in the case of suicide at the point of their physical death. But they have died many times over before their actual death because of the self-image that generated a chemical set within their body. Do you know that taking some anti-depressants bring on thoughts of suicide? This is because suicide is a chemical and not a decision. Both the old and what's new and next is always present and available.

Using this same point, most people do not have a decision-making issue, but they have a chemical issue in their body. Most psychologist focus on the mind, but accomplishment is about the body.

If you want something different in life and you want to achieve a specific goal, you must ask yourself, how bad do you want it? It's in our nature for things to die when we want something new, so what is it that has to be put to death? Does your dream die or do the things you don't need in life die? You have to put to death anything that's not aligned to what's on your mind that you want in life or you will die! This is what I mean by practicing death. Everyone does this daily whether they like it or not, whether they are conscious of it or not. Even when you experience what you don't want, it means something you do want that is meant for you to have has died. Death is always present. But what is it that is dying? Remember, every time you choose into something, you are choosing out of something at the same time.

Mind Make-Up

When sorrow or dissatisfaction is presented, the next move is to design something new. Again, some people use this point to go higher in life and gain more, and some people us this exact same point of decision-making to maintain or to merely survive from moment to moment. This is why you need an accounting of where you are, then you need a design along with your decision to be somewhere new, better and higher.

In order to get to your design, things that don't match your design need to die. You have to make-up your mind as death is a natural process of any type of mind make-up. When I say make up your mind, I do not mean in terms of making a decision. What I mean by making up your mind is that you have to make up your mind much like you make up a cake. You have to determine what goes into the mind, how it's mixed, and then matured, because once this is done, your mind is going to feed chemicals into your body with a matching image. That's why when people make up their minds (decision based) without making up their minds (development based), they never accomplish what they want to do.

When you do not make up your mind by design, there will always be lower energy forces available that will automatically become your mind make-up. This "make-up" is then set into your body as a chemical composition which in turn produces things in front of you for your experience. Once an image is set in your body as a chemical set, it is virtually unstoppable. This is the process of Spirit.

Energy Is an Equal Opportunity Worker

When you choose what doesn't work the same process takes place. Why? Physiologically when your mind has a certain build or makeup and when this makeup is not in your best interest, it still settles within your body. Since a responsive body always needs to produce after its kind or make-up, even the people, places, and things that are non-optimal towards what you really want in life become more important than what's best for you. Yes. What doesn't work then carries more value than what you know that does work.

Paul in the Christian Bible wrestled with this exact same condition:

Romans 7:15-20

¹⁵For that which I do I allow not: for what I would, that do I not; but what I hate, that do I.

¹⁶If then I do that which I would not, I consent unto the law that it is good.

¹⁷Now then it is no more I that do it, but sin that dwelleth in me.

¹⁸For I know that in me (that is, in my flesh,) dwelleth no good thing: for to will is present with me; but how to perform that which is good I find not.

¹⁹For the good that I would I do not: but the evil which I would not, that I do.

²⁰Now if I do that I would not, it is no more I that do it, but sin that dwelleth in me.

Romans 7:23-25

²³But I see another law in my members, warring against the law of my mind, and bringing me into captivity to the law of sin which is in my members.

²⁴O wretched man that I am! who shall deliver me from the body of this death?

25 I thank God through Jesus Christ our Lord. So then with the mind I myself serve the law of God; but with the flesh the law of sin.

Here Paul uses Jesus as the Image and a representation of an Image for success. You yourself have to come to the understanding that you are the Image that represents all the success that you can ever want. Jesus became Paul's point of focus as he had to deal with what his body was forcing upon him, kicking it back to his mind for assessment. Jesus then became a model for a corrected life view. This corrected life view delivered Paul from his life struggles. Your own corrected view of who you really are is the starting point of dealing with life's mind struggle and disappointment.

Notice this; some people believe that Jesus lived a life of poverty. If you believe that Jesus was relatively poor and struggled all through life, guess what? That becomes your life image. That's what will be built into your body. Yes. This erroneous belief becomes part of your mind makeup and you become successful at not making it or successful at experiencing a poor life existence. Most of religion today puts a bad spin on who you are personally and that you are "less than" and in need of "saving". It becomes even more terrible when they push the point by saying that Jesus was poverty stricken and killed to prove that your life can't be any better until you go to heaven.

The Point of This Book

It is important for me to address traditional religious beliefs in this book that are disempowering, because people need to move past their religious struggles and learn about the power allotted to every human being to make decisions and experience accomplishment beyond what's hurting them and beyond what brings on a deep sense of sorrow.

Note this: When your Faith follows your fear you still do incredible things; smoking is incredible, getting high is incredible, being physically and verbally abused is incredible, stressing yourself out until you are sick is incredible, eating to the point to where you lose your health is incredible, to struggle in life is an incredible feet, because your Faith will always produce more of what it is. That's why Faith is the substance and the evidence of what can't be seen, which in these instances is the fear that is being mirrored into your life. The opposite of fear is not Faith. The opposite of fear is function. You are either functioning or your fearful. Faith can be applied to either one. You can be faithfully fearful or you can be faithfully functioning.

You have to find within you the substance that extends beyond any condition. Everyman has it, but not every man gives it the attention needed. There is more to life than what you see in front of you, and that "more" starts in your mind.

Here's how you should outline it.

Faith is the substance that is built within you, literally. There is nothing wrong with fear. Fear is a reality of life, but you should follow after your fear with the Spirit of Faith and not follow after your Faith (that which is built within you) with the Spirit of fear. People who do great things despite surmounting odds become blinded to any obstacles because of the Image of what they want (substance) that is established within them. Their mind is so made up (development) that the chemicals in their body matches their mind, so they then walk with the feeling that they have already accomplished what they want.

Everyone uses the same psychological process of Faith in any venture whether it's to repeat an old habit or make a significant contribution to mankind, but the separation takes place in the mind makeup. Everything that is associated with your mind makeup should be growth components and not "hope to be" components. You have to ask the question, when I engage what is front of me, will it grow me, will it advance me, will it push me further, will I be at the next level afterwards etc. If it does not, you have to put it to death because it can quickly become part of your mind makeup. Everything has to reflect the Image of what you want in life from the people, the places, and the things that you choose. Everything has to speak to the Image inside you. I call these – Substantive Connections. Every connection you make must have substance.

1. Every choice in front of you is a connection not a direction.
2. Determine if that choice guarantees growth.
3. If not, put it to death.
4. Open yourself to choices that lead to growth.
5. Every choice has to reflect the success you want.
6. If you're still "hoping" after connecting, it's wrong.

Everything that is associated with your mind makeup should be growth components and not "hope to be" components.

When a mustard seed is planted, it will be what it is. When a lemon seed is planted, it will be what it is. When an apple seed is planted, it will be what it is. When a tomato seed is planted, it will be what it is. When an oak tree seed is planted, it will be what it is.

All minds work in the exact same way. We all do the impossible and the incredible, whether it's taking drugs or making a billion dollars. It all follows the same process and starts with the same starting gun. This start is the sensation of dissatisfaction and sorrow. But your mind makeup determines where you go after the meeting up with your sorrow, and your mind makeup determines your results. Your mind makeup is your seed or the substance within you.

Why do some live the lives that they want? Why do some people live a perpetual existence of survival or just getting by? Why do some people get what they want and some wish that they had? Ask yourself this. What is your personal energy poured into? Within every given moment you are adding to your life, multiplying your life, or you are maintaining, surviving, and losing into death.

Here's how it works.

The Concept of Sorrow

The concept of sorrow is fascinating. Sorrow is designed by God and leads to having more. What??? Sorrow allows you to have mastery and command over what you want in life. Let me prove it.

Sorrow is what you face when you deal with "what is not". It is a word that spans the multiplicity of circumstances that you face in the moments when you feel that things are not right, not complete, out of place, and unsatisfactory. Sorrow is rooted in the emotional system and speaks volumes as it is a response to your negative conditions. Sorrow was something that God told Eve that He would multiply in her life, and that when she would have children, it will be accompanied by sorrow. Many theologians marked this event as God cursing Eve and mankind in **Genesis 3**, but this perceived cursing is immediately negated by the factual comment made by God Himself, "Now man has become one of us" in verse 22. Could it be that sorrow was created for our benefit? Could it be that sorrow is a part of God's constitutional makeup?

Sorrow was not an institution that resulted from sin. Sorrow is a part of who God is and seems to come across as a privilege in Genesis 3 and not a curse. God said in **Genesis 3**,

1. **"I will multiply thy sorrow and thy conception."**
2. **"You shall bear children in sorrow."**
3. **"Now man has become as one of us."**

Never slight the order in which God Himself speaks. Where is the curse since man has been promoted into the Godhead? Take some time and look at this mystery a little closer.

Sorrow here is the prerequisite of doing something better. We generally misunderstand sorrow as it makes itself a present force in our lives. We feel sorrow when there is any type of loss or shortcoming. Many people have been brought to their knees by sorrow. But sorrow is a gift. Sorrow can be your best friend. As we image God, sorrow plays an important role in creation. But first, there must be a few things cleared up in what we know as the creation story.

The purpose of this book is to turn around long held beliefs that have imprisoned even the greatest minds of our time and throughout early Christian history. The Bible as it stands now, is the most widely read book in all of history. It has shaped the thoughts of many individuals, religious institutions, and denominations for hundreds of years. What surprises me with the Bible being such a standard and considered by most to be the Word of God, is that when most people read it, it doesn't catapult one's life into immediate success. You would think that success and prosperity would be the norm since it is "The Bible".

Since the Bible's canolitical discoveries, it has been subject not only to many interpretations, but also many translations by man, but yet it stands to be considered the "Word of God" which was in need of man's help to be translated so others can understand it. It might seem as though God purposefully came short of conveying His own Word, and then man was so blessed to be there to pick up the pieces to carry out this great work. Hmmmmm...

The Bible clearly says that, "Faith cometh by hearing, and hearing by the Word of God", but yet we insist on reading and not hearing.

Yes I said it! God's Word is better received by hearing which is the basis of Faith and not reading. So what's it all for anyway?

The point is, don't be so hard wired into versions of the Bible that you might think is "right", so much so that the Bible doesn't do you any good. Your reading can block your hearing and Faith cometh by hearing... **Ephesians 2:5** says that, "We are created unto Good works". So what good is it to believe in the Bible and its "man" interpreted versions if good works are not the result?

Everyone wants to lead a good life and live successfully. Everyone wants to experience good results. Everyone wants to think of what they love to have in life and actually get it. Luckily, the Bible does start with a narrative where God is doing just that. He's calling out the good and making it happen. What I am suggesting here is that you can effectively read the Bible and have the same experience, but you must listen for something also and not stake your whole life on a Biblical translation, which in a lot of cases simply stem from a man's opinion

My effort here is to clarify some long held beliefs that have caused many people to live their lives within the space of being "stuck". So I must point out some facts, make some interesting observations, dig into some more accurate definitions and interpretations of the Bible so you can find the freedom and empowerment that some of these scriptures really carry. Therefore when sorrow presents itself, it can be a fleeting moment as you will now be enabled to create over and above your sorrow. You can move from the "struggle" into the good that you are created for.

So throughout this book I will;

1. Point out a limiting beliefs in which I consider to be a misconception.
2. Provide you with an observation that can serve as a more corrected view.
3. Then show you how the corrected view can serve your success and prosperity and help you to master creating the things in life that you want.

Let's start with the creation story.

Limited Belief #1

The earth was created in seven literal 24 hour time periods comprising a week in time to create the entire universe. The truth is, is that earth was created in seven time periods that's not limited to a literal 24 hour day. Knowing this will help you in your journey of personal success.

Observation

It is clearly stated that the sun, moon, and stars in Genesis 1:8 was created to set the times and the seasons. Time did not exist until the 4th "day". Daahhh!!! How could there be a 24-hour time period when there was neither hours nor a measurement of time?

This leaves the door open to at least consider that the earth was created or better stated, unfolded in 13 billion years as nature through scientific revelation has proved. To me, it makes for a better creation story. It takes nothing away from God for scientist to discover how God created or unfolded the earth over time.

If you notice, very carefully, in the first parts of the creation narrative, God did a lot of dividing. He divided the waters from the waters. He divided the firmaments. He divided the sea from the land, and this process of divisions continues throughout Earth's development. Pay close attention to this observation. In Genesis 1 you are really reading a story of divisions and not creation. You are reading a story of unfolding. When people think that God popped everything into existence in twinklings of moments, God is viewed as a "Mr. Magic "pop-up" God" versus a true Creator. Why is this important?

Glad you asked? When you use the words "divided from", then everything that exists came out of a single source and then divided. So as something new is developed, it is developed from what already existed. It is more accurate to read Genesis 1 this way,

In the beginning God created the Heavens and the Earth.

DONE!

Now He takes what was created and begins to divide it into more. By the way, He did the same thing when He fed the 5000. He took the little boys lunch and divided it into more. Now it sounds like scientific history is a little bit more on the money here. The substance from which everything is derived came from one point in history, and then the totality of that substance rest in every human being.

In the beginning God created, BANG! DONE! Now what was so little was divided into more over time, and this division then becomes provision. So we see systems of provisions being instituted into all of creation. You have the biological trophic system where one part of earth's existence supports and becomes a supply for other parts of existence. Let's not make this difficult. We see it every day. The earth provides for the earth. Notice that one trophic system is only 10% of the previous trophic system that supports it. So "supply" is a key characteristic of creative development.

How does this help you?

Since we now know that there weren't six days of new things "popping up" each day, we are left with the realization that things are actually birthed out of things. God was dividing and then multiplying (the process of unfolding), and then He gave us the commandment in Genesis 2, to be fruitful and multiply. Multiply from what? Multiply from what's already in you. Within you, you contain the entirety of creation. Every level of creation lives to prove that existence is birthed out of existence.

Anybody who says that they don't have what it takes to accomplish something that they desire in life is lying to themselves, because how can you not accomplish what you want with everything literally existing within you! Everything that has ever been in existence is faithfully supplied by previous existences. It all started from you. It is hard to grasp this if you think that these existences popped up separately with no relation to previous existences.

Everybody is scared of the premise that man came from monkeys, but if God made the monkeys to get you here, what difference does it make? It's like baking a beautiful wedding cake, but denying the flour that it took to make the cake. Most Christians want to believe that God popped us into existence on a specific day, but you have to realize that all of existence is God and all of existence is you. I do not mind that God used the process of birthing from primordial beginnings of minute substances to get to His final product, me!

Primarily, the relationship is that of being birthed out of a previous existence is the basis for all relationships. It is vitally important to grasp this observation of "birth". The biblical translations we use today reads, "divided from", but "divided from" is the same thing as birthing. When a mother gives birth to a child, as it is born, it is a new entity, but it is divided from the mother and as yet, it is still related to the mother.

Everything from the beginning of the universe is related to you as the earth over many years gave birth to new existences until you showed up. Then every previous existence is also a supply to the next. With you being at the far end of the food chain, you are fully provided for and you are fully supplied for to gain every kind of desire and level of success.

I don't read Genesis 1 in a mamsy-pansy or elementary way. I match it up with Psalms 139, which states that, "We are fearfully and wonderfully made". Our personal troubles come from whether we know this or not.

The Legacy of Sorrow

Let's get back to the word sorrow - the word that should be our friend. Sorrow was a part of the process of earth's development way before man sinned. Sorrow, when it makes itself present is a signal that it is time for you to move beyond where you currently are to a new place in life. It is at this point you should be encouraged to grow into more by dividing from (separating from what's older - death) and multiplying into more. You are designed to unfold.

Limiting Belief #2

Death and Sorrow entered into the earth once Adam and Eve sinned. It is believed that Adam and Eve's disobedience caused death and sorrow to enter into God's creation. The truth is, is that death was and is a part of God's order and structure. Knowing this and being aware of how this plays a role in your life today will benefit your growth tremendously.

Observation

Genesis 1:6 states that vegetation was birthed into existence –
which is the Third Day in Genesis. This introduces a process that is
continued today in a very unique way. You have as a part of this day
trees that provide fruit, and then you have the herbs of the field. In
order to increase, there had to be a point of division and separation. In
every herb and tree that bear fruit there are seeds. Seeds contain the
potential of a whole pasture or orchard within itself. The total purpose
of a seed is to be planted, grow into new existences after its kind, and
then multiplied into even more. In order to do this, the seed has to die in
order to be rebirthed into more. Notice, there is a type of death that
exists within this process.

When God told Adam and Eve, that if they should partake of the
fruit of the tree of Knowledge of Good and Evil, He said to them, "you
shall surely die". Again, most approach this part of the narrative as a
sentence on the lives of Adam and Eve, and thusly believe that their
disobedience introduced death to mankind. Can you imagine? You and
I never got a chance to sin for ourselves in order to be punished? How
ludicrous is an idea such as that?

My poor brother. He was the oldest of three children. Whenever we were left at home, my brother, being the oldest would always get
punished for stuff he did and the stuff my sister and I did also. Even
when he didn't do anything, if something in the house was broken, he
got the spanking. I loved my parent's philosophy! My brother gets the
beating for my mess ups. Are we really naturally punished because of
Adam and Eve's disobedience? Come on folks, let's grow up!

If you can pull yourself away for a moment from the elementari-
ness of it all, do you really think God would order a punishment for all
mankind for one person's mistake? We seem to think so based on
Romans 5:12-21 which is grossly misread.

What most do here is cut the story short and miss the latter part
of this text. "Where sin abounds, grace much more abound" needs to be
the focal point of this reading. Based on Romans 5:12, sin entered the
world and then death by sin. So there is a death that is a natural order

that leads to new life, and then there is a death brought on by sin. Both deaths are present at every decision-making juncture.

If one was to read a little further into Genesis versus stopping at **Genesis 2:17**, "you shall surely die", and then read further through Genesis chapter 3, you will actually find out that Adam and Eve weren't sentenced to just a death, but they were also sentenced to have the same knowledge that God had. Man was not cursed to "death" as we know it and understand it, man was blessed to an advanced knowledge. This knowledge is not just the knowledge of good and evil, but more correctly stated, the knowledge of the good that exist beyond evil. This is the knowledge of "more" and the knowledge of the good that exist beyond your sorrow. "Ye shall surely die". Get it?

Every seed must die to grow into more based on the knowledge that exists within the "seed". If you partake of the fruit of this tree "you shall surely die" – but "now man has become as one of Us", Genesis 3:22. But this leaves us with two conditions; death into what's dying or death into more. We choose. Both choices take the same amount of energy, but in both ways you die and you die daily. This is the practice of death.

How does this help you?

Dissatisfaction is the key here. The key to dissatisfaction is that dissatisfaction and sorrow should lead to more. More is staple to all of life. Growth and production rest at the heart of the Universe and at the heart of every human being. Moving on to "more" is a natural process built within the infrastructure of all life. The whole narrative of development in Genesis 1 is about life being birthed into more on a daily basis. Everything unfolds into more.

In order to move onto more, you have to be dissatisfied or be sorrowful with what currently exist. This is what you might call a necessary evil. But you are designed to see the good beyond it (the knowledge of good and evil, the knowledge of good beyond evil). Wanting more is always based on that which is current not being enough. This is a good thing. Without the emotion of dissatisfaction and sorrow, everything would remain stagnant. Nothing would unfold. So we see this in **Genesis 1**. God never stated, "And it was good" until after He created "more".

Interestingly enough, He proclaimed that "it was good" 5 times and then "it was not good" 1 time.

What?

Yes. Before Adam and Eve "sinned", there was something that "was not good" that existed. So before "sin", there was life and death, good and not good, good and evil, so Adam and Eve's disobedience did not introduce death and sorrow. So, what was not good? It was not good for man to be alone. Man needed a helpmeet to produce more. Once Eve came onto the scene, they were commanded to be fruitful and multiply. Move onto "more".

So, how does this help you? Life is about more. Every human being within the circumstances and moments of life wants more. If more is not achieved, one is left with a sense of deficiency and dissatisfaction. Not a good feeling to have. But you are actually designed to bypass this state of "less", which is evil. At every juncture in life you are faced with the following alternating conditions: joy and sorrow, life and death, love and fear, sin and grace. I want you to consciously be aware of these 4 alternating conditions that every life circumstance will cause you to face.

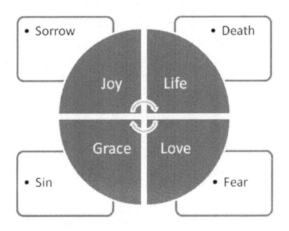

Here you choose where to cycle your personal energy. I mean just that, at every juncture, you choose and direct your personal energy. In every moment you are faced with these opposites of existence. You will always be faced with the knowledge of good and evil, or batter stated, the good that exists beyond evil.

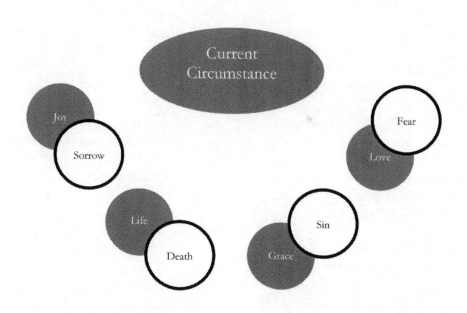

Your mind is just like an airport terminal. Whenever you have a thought of a goal or a desire, other thoughts will fly in and land at that same terminal. If you entertain any other flight options besides what you have decided, you will be taken in an entirely different direction.

I call these choices **"the possibility of state"**. We choose into what's next based on our state. But based on the modern Christian belief system and values, most think our default state is sin and death, so we approach life naturally with fear which then results into more sorrow - and so we cycle on. We cycle consistently into what we don't want, which leaves what we do want in this life a distant dream. Somehow this has been made to be ok, because we are then comforted with the idea that if we aren't quite happy, we will get a reward once we die and go to heaven. This is total bull and I'm so sorry that so many people pay their money to well-meaning churches, but never see any real and substantive improvement in their lives!

Joy, Life, Love and Grace is our default state and it is our natural state. Adam and Eve did not mess this up. We are only taught that. Dissatisfaction is natural, but it is not meant to be used as an order to go into a state of fear which then introduces a death that you don't want.

God used the system of dissatisfaction and sorrow to move you to the next level. Yes. How can you want more without being dissatisfied with what is less? In order to move on to more, you have to put what is less to death. Seeds die in order to become orchards. This is the first and original type of death. This is the process of evolution that existed after creation and is still in place today.

Fossilization

Things that do not move on into "more", fossilizes and is then used as fertilizer and fuel for that which is more advanced. This is the second type of death. Ignorance leads to fossilization. What do you do when you are faced with a situation that you are not happy with? You GROW! This is who God is, God is growth. But sometimes you might stand in what you don't like and then fossilize into that state leaving you dead, yet while you are still alive.

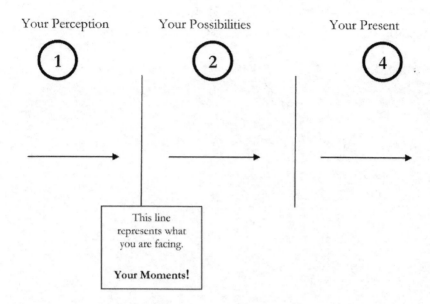

At every moment you can either live or die. Let me show you where Eve died, and by understanding this you can keep yourself from dying. Your life results are determined not just by how you see and view your possibilities, but by how you see and view yourself. Here is where Eve made her mistake. Eve heard from the serpent that if she ate the fruit she would be like God. The error in her perception was that she did not factor into the equation that she was made in the Image of God, therefore she was already like God to begin with. Eve had reduced herself in her own mind, which then lead her to eating the fruit to make up the difference. This act left Adam and Eve living in dead results. This second death that happens above ground is horrible because you are dead while you are yet alive. When you do not see yourself correctly, you become a fossil.

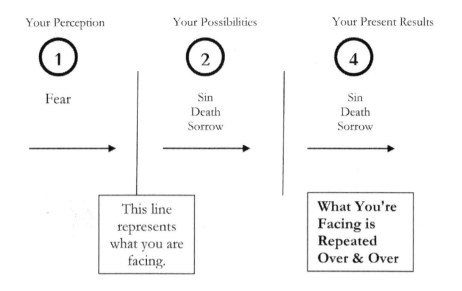

God before then always used dissatisfaction or sorrow to create better results and a greater existence. Death was used to bury what was old in order to make room for what was new and next. Eve viewed herself and then became dissatisfied with herself. Then instead of death being projected upon what needed to die so she could grow as she faced the serpent, she became subject to her own view-point and perception of herself, then all her future possibilities followed suit. Death was then projected onto her and she became fossilized. This is not a sentence imposed by God, but a state of being chosen by Eve.

Project love onto yourself. Life and death starts with what you think about yourself. That's why it said in Proverbs that, "Life and Death is in the power the tongue". Life and death is in the power of how your personal sound is projected from yourself. Your unsatisfactory circumstances are meant to die, not you. Love projected on others is just that, love. Love projected on yourself is perfect love. Perfect love starts with a correct image of yourself. So when you are faced with circumstances that you want to change, you do not need to focus on the image of what's wrong in front of you, but you focus on your self-image. This will

help you to master what you want in life and command your good
results. You have to build a correct self-image.

Here are some scriptures that will help:

2 Timothy 1:7

*For God hath not given us the spirit of fear; but of power, and of love, and of a sound
mind.*

1 John 4:18

*There is no fear in love; but perfect love casteth out fear: because fear hath torment. He
that feareth is not made perfect in love.*

2 Corinthians 5:4

*For we that are in [this] tabernacle do groan, being burdened: not for that we
would be unclothed, but clothed upon, that death might be swallowed up of life.*

Romans 5:20

*Moreover the law entered, that the offence might abound. But where sin
abounded, grace did much more abound:*

Psalms 30:5

*For his anger [endureth but] a moment; in his favour [is] life: weeping may
endure for a night, but joy [cometh] in the morning.*

Growing From Small to Big

What is very interesting is how religious beliefs, especially within the Western society, have affected how we view the mind and spirituality. I want to note here, that not all religious people are successful. Not all religious people can master and command what they want in their life. It would seem that since we are dealing with religion and God, that more people would be successful in life. So what is it that is believed that keeps a good number of people that are religious in a perpetual struggle from day-to-day even though they go to church week after week? Many people are waiting for God to move in their situations. Religion becomes a matter of how to get God to make the right move, but the Bible states that, "In Him, _we move_ and have our being".

This chapter is not a challenge to the religious norms within to-day's society, but I want to use some of our current religious beliefs as a backdrop to the early Genesis narrative in order to bring a greater understanding as to how the Word works, the meaning of sound, and how it relates to your success.

The "You" That Exist Beyond "You"

There seems to be this insatiable need to be low, feel low, and to be undervalued. Feeling low for the most part is a safety mechanism for those who can't explain life or figure out a way to escape their failures in life. Primarily, the thought is, is that if you start with a low mind-set, complete with the corresponding low feelings, you can successfully deal with life's disappointments, and life's failures can then become manageable.

Many people live well below their God given potential, and sometimes today's religions actually set the environment for this type of lack-luster living. A good number of people miss the fact that they are way more than they think they are or give themselves credit to be. What in the world do I mean by this?

Human potential is unlimited, but a lot of people have found a way to live within limitations. As human beings, we are way more than we give ourselves credit to be. We have hidden our greatest selves in a dark closet because of the fear of loss and the fear of death. Most people are fighting to protect and to preserve the puniest life existence. This is because they live with the mindset that all that they have in life is their immediate surroundings in which most count to be insufficient. So people fight to protect the little that they have.

Protecting the little and preserving the little is all done at the expense of our greater selves.

For the most part, today's major religious institutions play a major role in authenticating the smallness and shortness of this little life that we are "privileged with", so we do everything we can not to lose it.

There seems to be this big God, and then there is the little people on earth who are left with the only option of making sure this big God stays pleased. This creates a perpetual existence of survival, and for the most part, a great number of people miss the opportunity to live great lives when this is their engrained focus. Energy is sapped up trying to be like this big God in order to win His approval, or more importantly, trying to be "good" for God. We don't want to mess up or God will exact "loss" upon our lives. This is the basic tenant of most religious settings.

What is missed here is, is that being made in the image of God seems to tell me that you are who He is. Yes, equal to God! But how afraid are most religions of that?

Philippians 2:5-6

Let this mind be in you, which was also in Christ Jesus: Who, being in the form of God, thought it not robbery to be equal with God:

Religious Ideas versus The Mind

Most people believe in a higher power and this higher power has many references. It all depends on what religious persuasion you come from or what belief system you hold that determines what and who this higher power is. Most of today's protestant churches claim to have a lock on the doings and movements of this great God. But somehow a great God automatically denotes that His subjects, the people on earth, are less than who God is by default. "Don't dare to express yourself as being higher than the definition God has imposed on you! That is blasphemous!", some would say.

So people start with the ideology that there is this big old God who made us little, itty-bitty humans, and we ought to stay in our place. This forces an imprisoning mindset of being "less than".

This is a dangerous equation!

Limited Belief #3

Humans are part of God's Creation. It has always been understood that God made man on the sixth day as a part of His creation. God did not make man. God made man in His image. To state this in a more clear way, God reflected His image into creation which is you and I. You and I existed in one state before the foundation of the world and was then reflected into an operative state that we see today.

Observation

May I submit to you here that we grossly misunderstand the phrase "let Us make man in Our image" found in the book of Genesis in the Christian Bible. There are two key words here, and we subconsciously use one word to cancel out the other. We tend to focus on the supposed fact that we were "made", but the word "image" conflicts with the word "made". Can you actually make an image? No. An image is subject to the fact that something already exists in order for there to be an image. So if we think we are "made", then we must also think of ourselves as being less than our maker. But if we are an actual image or a reflection of something, then our image is "made" by what is already in existence becoming visible. You and I are not made but reflected. You might not get this in a traditional religion.

So "made", in this case, doesn't denote being made from scratch, but simply becoming a visible form of what was already in existence. So the idea here is that you are the visible form of who God is. What is actually made is a reflection. It is important here at this point to understand that there is an existence that exists in fullness, and anything that is "made" is not actually "made", but reflected.

"What in the hell...!!!???", you might ask.

Most of today's religions, especially in the West would reject this notion, thinking; aren't we so messed up, so evil, we can't get things right, we make mistakes, get sick, cheat, lie, steal...? How can this be? Are we not "less than" God because of these things? If truly, at one time we were like God, didn't Adam and Eve mess that up for all of us?

Man, that's some real power. Can one woman really eat a piece of fruit and mess up the whole human race?!?? If so, then this one act becomes the most powerful act ever! This would then make Eve superhuman, having the power to screw up all of mankind in one bite. And so we believe. And poor us. Poor struggling mankind. Waahh, Waahh, Waahh! Now we need a Religious Baby Bottle so we can at least get a sensation that we are all ok.

We are like an infant, needing God to "feed" us because we deem ourselves as helpless humans and God will cater to our needs if we are good enough or "favored". This completely knocks out the truth of "we are who He is" and replaces it with the ideal that God messed up by making a faulty existence called the Human Being, and we are all included in this major global experiment that went awry. Now because of this human error that God made, we need to meet every week to pay homage to this big God, learn to do right, or get zapped. Somehow this seems to make people comfortable. That's what we need, comfort; and this religious baby bottle seems to do the trick. In a lot of cases, people's lives do not seem to improve while they are comforted by these religious beliefs.

It is said "Stop crying about life. God's going to "fix" it. By the way leave me a check before you leave church". Some are very afraid to ask the question, "Does my religious beliefs improve my life, or do I hang on to the supposed fact that one day God will make it better, even if it means dying first and getting my reward in heaven at a later time?" Is this really who God is?

Most people are comfortable with the idea of being less than who God is. Less than the Universal Intelligence. Less than our true beginnings. Less than who we are called to be. Less than our true image. Less than our true potency. People become religious about their self-imposed limitations and look for weekly church satisfaction to validate their imposed lowliness along with comfortable catch phrases such as, "God - nobody is greater than you", and "Only God is worthy", and within this, we lose our own self-worth. Somehow it is believed that in making ourselves "less than", we appease this big God, and then from that point we are then loved.

You can readily see how this causes an expansive and explosive psychosis. This is how a good number of people deal with the world around them. Be "less than" so you can win approval and thusly be loved. But if you are an image, a reflected image, are you really less than? No, you are not! You and I are a reflection.

How does this help you?

The "You" Outside of "You"

Be afraid. Be very afraid. But I don't really have to tell you that. Most people are afraid of their true selves anyhow. When they get a sensation of something more, they back up from the uncharted territory of their greater selves.

Over "there" is scary. This is the domain of the gods! Keep the hell out!

"I need you to be less so I can keep my "god" status", saith the Lord! Don't find out who you really are.

The truth is, all humans have an unlimited presence, and everything within the expanse of the presence of every individual is infinite. I call this, the "You" Outside of "You", and I can use a point of proof by reminding you of the fact that we are made in God's image. If God is omnipresent, then we being made as an image must also be more than our physical presence. You and I are unlimited and infinite within the structures that extend from us.

God never made anyone with a "period" at the end!

May I submit to you that our "messing up" is just our inability to handle the belief in what extends outside of ourselves. Our messing up is rooted in believing that we are less. Knowing the reflective characteristics of reality as reality starts it's reflection from what can't be seen is paramount to understanding how to reflect your own unseen thoughts into reality.

But of course, there is a great sense of inability that lurks here. This is because what you don't know does hurt you. Or better stated, what you decide not to know can and will hurt you. Let's look again at Eve and the fruit.

The Christian account of "the fall of man" states that Eve was told that if she partakes of the fruit, she would then "be like God". At this point, what Eve decided not to realize, is that being an "image" of who God is, meant she was already like God - an image, a reflection. Therefore, she ate the fruit in the attempt to become who she already was. Isn't that the basis of all psychosis? It is the non-recognition of who you are, then the subsequent attempts to make up the difference at any cost?

To be or not to be is not the question. You are, is the answer.

Now you can plan not to live below who you are and what's available to you. You weren't condemned to a life of lowliness because of Adam and Eve. Outside of what they thought of themselves, you can think higher because you are not subject to what happened to them. You are not sentenced to doom and struggle, because "that's just the way it is". As a matter of fact, this becomes an excuse for poverty and low thinking. Because of one man's sin, we are all sinners. This is not true. You and I are not living in a "fallen state". Let's take a closer look.

Limiting Belief #4

When Adam and Eve partook of the fruit it was "the fall of man". It is highly considered that every man exist within a fallen state. The truth is, the Bible never mentions man as "fallen", and furthermore it never mentions that man is in a "fallen" state. Where did this come from? The truth is, you did not exist in a fallen state. To know this as the truth will give you a clear idea as to your true nature in God which can then lead to a greater understanding of your purpose.

Observation

Low evaluation of yourself will always be mirrored against your true status, thusly giving rise to the need to be better, and a good bit of this is done at a major cost and unnecessary sacrifice. First, there is no such thing as the "fall of man", it was only at this point that Adam and Eve became aware of the option of "less than" and then they subsequently built a relationship to "less than". Man did not fall in the beginning; man only refocused his attention and became exposed to another option. There is no such thing as "I can't", it can only be you focusing on what can't be done, because what can be done is always there. You decide what you are exposed to by what you place your mind on and where you place your attention. Diminished options to our true desire is the real enemy.

Eve chose to expose herself to an inability. Her status with God never changed, only her state of mind changed. When something is not working for you in life, you are dealing with a state of being and not a status of being. It is never that you can't do something, because the "can" is always there. What are you tied into that gives you the sense of "can't"? When you change the idea of "can't", you will instantly change your state, which will then match your status. Stop exposing yourself to inabilities.

Men don't fail; men only choose to see differently, and then live in what they only perceive to be a failure.

You are Complete

Man looks to feel complete. In order to feel complete his sense of completeness must be mirrored from a complete state, and this complete state is just as much of a reality than physical reality. So, there is a need to experience substance and to gain a sense of completeness. You will find within the Genesis account in the Christian Bible, substance was fully provided for everyone, which is your Faith. Faith in what? Faith in who you are? Without knowing who you are, it is hard to feel substantive or have faith. This is why substance abuse is so prevalent. People are trying to get what they already have, go where they already are, and to be who they are already created to be by using off-balanced relationships with people and substances to make up the difference. People are then left feeling empty, along with the content of their souls being continuously drained.

Without knowing who you are, it is difficult to have faith.

Every soul is full, but somehow we have learned to experience an empty state, not realizing that every individual is infinite and unlimited. It is the "You" that extends outside of "You". Everything in the Universe is completed and connected within you, which makes you a correct image of the Divine. Scientists are now discovering this fact more and more everyday as they research the human biological make-up and its psychological structures. Most of the foremost business leaders, great thinkers, and world trend-setters tap into this very fact every day and consistently retrieve into their lives "what's next".

Isn't this who God is? Isn't this the chief characteristic of The Universal. How is it that our minds do not pick up on this fact and we thusly live "less than" or live powerless lives?

The answer to this is found in Genesis Chapter 3. This narrative is supposed to outline the details of the "fall of man" and God's subsequent conversation with Adam and Eve. But what's surprising here is that there is absolutely no mention of the "fall of man" in Genesis, nor can you find it anywhere else in the Bible.

So what did happen? Let's start here.

Genesis 3:8

And they heard the voice of the LORD God walking in the garden in the cool of the day: and Adam and his wife hid themselves from the presence of the LORD God amongst the trees of the garden.

And they heard the Voice walking. The sound of God approached Adam and Eve walking in the garden. The Voice walked. But they hid themselves. Why? What was up with the Voice? If the Voice walking was God and they were made in His image, then the Voice also reflected who they were. Adam and Eve was hiding from their own truth. The sound or the voice was a representation of their completeness Who they were, scared them.

Genesis 3:9-11

⁹ And the LORD God called unto Adam, and said unto him, Where art thou?

¹⁰ And he said, I heard thy voice in the garden, and I was afraid, because I was naked; and I hid myself.

¹¹ And he said, Who told thee that thou wast naked? Hast thou eaten of the tree, whereof I commanded thee that thou shouldest not eat?

"Naked" in the original Hebrew means to be ashamed. It was a self-evaluation of his condition as Adam stood in judgment of himself just like Eve did earlier. That's why God asked, "Who told you that you were naked? You've must have been around that tree that's telling you something different". What are the trees and serpents in your life that is telling you something different.? Again, man did not fall, but simply gained different knowledge.

Notice as you read the next 9 versus through verse 19, God chooses to curse the serpent and then He chooses to curse the ground. Notice God never cursed Adam and Eve. Here's what He actually tells Eve:

Genesis 3:16

Unto the woman he said, I will greatly multiply thy sorrow and thy concep-tion; in sorrow thou shalt bring forth children; and thy desire [shall be] to thy husband, and he shall rule over thee.

So now we are back at this word "sorrow". He's going to multi-ply thy sorrow and thy conception. And in "sorrow" you shall bring forth children. As I stated in the first chapter, sorrow or dissatisfaction is a tool for creation. It means to labor. He also says He's going to multiply thy conception, which means progenitor or originator. Notice God says them together. Again, Sorrow means "labor". God Himself labored for six days before He rested. Let me help you align this,

Exodus 20:9

Six days shalt thou labour, and do all thy work:

Labor comes before birth, then there is rest. Many people, when they want something, they don't want it bad enough. When you really want something bad enough you labor for it. Most people wait on God to make a move and miss the fact that we are blessed to labor. We look for God to answer when we are the answer.

Matthew 11:28

Come unto me, all [ye] that labour and are heavy laden, and I will give you rest.

Labor comes before rest or success. People wait for God to "work it out" when the work is our responsibility.

God labored for six days based on sorrow, stopping, evaluating, and then creating bigger and better as the days progressed. Now do you see what God multiplied. He wasn't cursing Eve, He was advancing Eve into this new knowledge of "evil" that actually wakes you up to what's good or what's next. Here's what God said to Adam:

Genesis 3:17-19

17 And unto Adam he said, Because thou hast hearkened unto the voice of thy wife, and hast eaten of the tree, of which I commanded thee, saying, Thou shalt not eat of it: cursed is the ground for thy sake; in sorrow shalt thou eat of it all the days of thy life;

18 Thorns also and thistles shall it bring forth to thee; and thou shalt eat the herb of the field;

19 In the sweat of thy face shalt thou eat bread, till thou return unto the ground; for out of it wast thou taken: for dust thou art, and unto dust shalt thou return.

Again, God is not cursing Adam, God cursed the ground for Adam's sake and then in "sorrow", Adam shall eat of it all the days of his life. The ground has become a specific place of provision for Adam in which he has to labor. Notice Adam will return to the ground in which he came from. Since Adam came from the ground, Adam will be actually eating from and by His own potential. Your potential does not start from a finished product, your potential starts as a seed...cursed is the ground. Now you labor to get results.

Isaiah 65:22

They shall not build, and another inhabit; they shall not plant, and another eat: for as the days of a tree [are] the days of my people, and mine elect shall long enjoy the work of their hands.

Now, let's look at a final statement made by God:

Genesis 3:22

And the LORD God said, Behold, the man is become as one of us, to know good and evil:

Here is another way of putting **Genesis 3:22**. Knowing good and evil is to know what you want and then having the ability to push past any evil to obtain it. Good is seeing what you want beyond what you don't want, and then doing what it takes to make it happen – labor.

So, God says here, "Man has become as one of us".

So where in this narrative do you find the "fall of man"? Most people do not accomplish what they want in life because they are "waiting on God" instead of laboring towards what they want.

How does this help you?

Let's start with the voice or sounds. Your possibilities are voiced by defining entities. Let us...make...Let us labor. If you made a list of things you may have done during the course of the day, you might be surprised as to how much you do not labor towards what you want in life. Most people, instead of being sorrowful which Biblically means to labor, they become sorry.

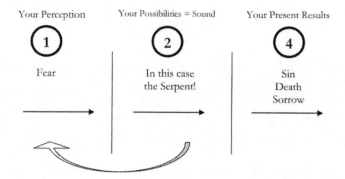

What Eve heard here was the serpent from the tree and then fear was introduced. But fear was also the subject when Adam heard the Voice walking in the garden. They hid themselves. They were afraid of their own Sound walking towards them. They were afraid of their own potential and possibilities. They were afraid of their own image. So, you can have both an Image issue and a Sound issue at the same time.

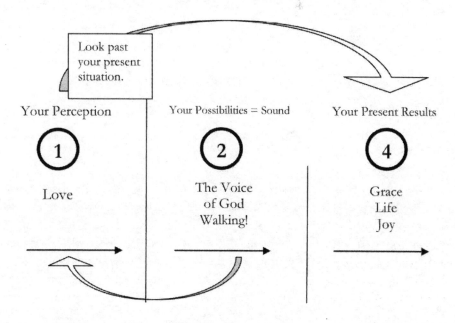

You have to allow the Sound of God to walk into your perception. When you see or experience something that you are not satisfied with, you have a mind and the right to see differently, and then you can choose to hear differently. God asked Adam, "Who told you that you were naked?" Have you been at that tree listening to that other voice?

When you want to drive a nicer car, but you said couldn't afford it, who told you that you couldn't?

When you wanted to start a new business, but you said you didn't have the education, who told you that?

When you wanted to move into a nicer neighborhood or move into a bigger home and you said that isn't for me, who told you that?

When you wanted a promotion on your job and you said they will never promote me, who told you that?

Have you been at that tree again listening to the voice of the serpent about who you are not? Who told you that you were naked?

The point of the narrative in **Genesis 3** is to bring out the fact that you do not have to reduce your self-image to match the sounds of the naysayer, but there is a walking Voice that is fully present to you with a full picture of who you are. Stop hiding from the Sound of God! Stop hiding from your truth.

You are who God is and nothing less! Who told you that you weren't?

Within this, these questions might come up... If our existence is so expansive and a reflection of the Divine, why don't we know everything? Why don't we have all the answers? Why can't I with one thought or one word make things right in my life or make things better? Since I can't do that, God must be" greater than" and I am "less than".

Well, let me ask you a few questions? If God is greater, why doesn't He just do all those things for you? He's God. Hmmmmmmm...?

Why doesn't He just say the one magic word and everything in your life pops right into place? Why does He just not feed all the starving people in the world and call it a day? Why doesn't He just give everybody some real money so there is no need to steal and embezzle? Why doesn't He just walk into every hospital and make everybody well? Hmmmmmm? It seems as though God's status at getting anything done runs a little parallel to ours.

At this point, this book might hit quite a few garbage cans. How dare you question God!!!?

Well, how dare you question yourself!!!?

How dare you deny who you are?

From this point on, the faint of heart should cease reading this book. I will employ a biblical text in the second chapter of the Book of Philippians, "Let this mind be in you, which was also in Christ Jesus, who thought it not robbery to be equal to God".

What???!!!?

Limiting Belief #5

We are less than who God is. This is a worldwide proclamation of most Christians and other religious dogmas. The truth is, is that every man is a constant and consistent reflection of who God is. The awareness of this is being masked for the benefit of religion. To know your true standing in God can give a greater sense of how you can move past your present conditions as you realize that your higher state remains complete by the Word of God.

Observation

Growth and Growing

We are asked here to have the same mind as God, along with the beginning thought, to be equal with Him. Is this a biblical stretch or what? The answer is no. The true seed of who you are lies in waking up to a greater knowledge. Growth is staple to all existence, and experience is about moving from one existence to greater existences. More, and having more is central to all life, even the life of God.

**Mankind does not have an "evil" problem,
but a "sleeping" problem; asleep to what's "more".**

Let's go back to the tough questions about our ability and God's ability to make things right. Notice, whether you believe the biblical account of creation, the scientific account of the big bang theory along with evolution, or as a great number people now currently do, they believe that evolution and creation are one and the same event; despite your foundation, all of these stories begin with a small beginning, or as the Bible states, began with an earth that was without form and void. Either way, both grew throughout time to where we are now in Earth's history - into more. This fact is clear, that even God or the Universal Intelligence, whatever or whomever He is to you, He chose not to start with everything. The Universe and God Himself started with something small and unstable and grew it into more.

"More" is the purpose of life.

How does this help you?

Here it is...

Whatever state or condition you are in, you can always reach another state or a greater state, which in turn changes your condition. Even in the Bible, the Hebrew translation of "without form and void" as found in **Genesis 1** is chaos. So where did chaos come from? Where did the "without form and void" come from? If the universe began as a small spec exploding into a massive existence, and then within billions of years evolved into what we see now, why did God start with a small spec? Where did the "small" come from?

Small is never a problem. Where you decide to grow from the "small" is what's important. Void is not an issue. How you decide to fill the void can be the issue. Chaos is not a problem, how you decide to grow over and above chaos should be your focus.

Here is where we miss-define God. Here is where we dub the Universal Intelligence wrong. Here is where we make an erroneous description of the Spirit. Fullness is not about being complete, because fullness never really reaches a state of completion. The Universe is always in a state of growth and expansion. There is always more. Fullness is about recognizing your ablility.

Fullness is about your ability to grow. Small, void, chaos, or things not being right, does exist, but it does not mean that you are without the ability to grow. You can grow from any point. That's the point of God, Spirit, or the Universal Intelligence – the ability to grow. You can grow from any point. It is your ability to grow that is the image of the Divine, not your size. So growing is a responsibility.

You are intricately designed to grow.

Psalms 139:16

Thine eyes did see my substance, yet being unperfect; and in thy book all [my members] were written, [which] in continuance were fashioned, when [as yet there was] none of them.

Limiting Belief #6

Our life starts at birth, and the life of mankind started when God blew into man's nostrils the breath of life. This is a minor over sight. The truth is, God blowing into man the breath of life denotes that life existed before in order for God to blow it into man. Quite simple. And man became a living soul…there's that change in state that I mentioned earlier. "And man became"…denotes…"And man was" in order to become. So life always is, but living can be turned on and off. You decide the state. If you are not alive, you can become alive. God's Spirit is always present.

Observation

Ephesians 1:3-6

³Blessed be the God and Father of our Lord Jesus Christ, who hath blessed us with all spiritual blessings in heavenly places in Christ:

⁴According as he hath chosen us in him before the foundation of the world, that we should be holy and without blame before him in love:

⁵Having predestinated us unto the adoption of children by Jesus Christ to himself, according to the good pleasure of his will,

⁶To the praise of the glory of his grace, wherein he hath made us accepted in the beloved.

So, we can clearly see here that we are chosen in God before the foundation of the world. Don't mean to shock ya. But you are not a pop-up presence as some believe that all the Universe is. You have always been life blessed with all spiritual blessings. But the key here is "in heavenly places".

1 Corinthians 15:49

And as we have borne the image of the earthy, we shall also bear the image of the heavenly.

Ephesians 2:6-7

⁶And hath raised us up together, and made us sit together in heavenly places in Christ Jesus:

⁷That in the ages to come he might shew the exceeding riches of his grace in his kindness toward us through Christ Jesus.

Colossians 3:3

For ye are dead, and your life is hid with Christ in God.

So why are we in so much trouble? Remember that word sorrow. God Himself chose to start with trouble. Remember the word "sorrow". Sorrow will always be a beginning point to greatness. Where ever you are in life, it is a starting point.

From Small to Big, From Nothing to Something

One generally deals with their psychosis by addressing the local issue of what's wrong in the moment versus spending time constructing their solutions in heavenly places, which then allows one to grow over and above undesired states. Everyone has a Spirit that is infinite and is in a constant relationship to other subsequent minds that are also infinite. This is God's Spirit, and in the Genesis account of our earth's history, the Spirit hovered over the waters which were without form and void. So here, there were two presences that existed at the same time. One is chaos (without form and void), and then the other is the Spirit of God that exist over and above that which was without form and void. The Spirit through sound was able to take that which was small and without form and void, reshaped it and then grew it. The Spirit of God never dies or goes away.

So plainly stated, "In the beginning God created the heavens and the earth and the earth was without form and void." You were chosen in God before the beginning, so the state of "without form and void" does not affect your position, nor does it affect your potential outcomes.

God, the Universal Intelligence, the Spirit of God started, with "without"!

So "without" can't be a bad place to start, because it is still who God is and it is a place where the Universal Intelligence Himself decided to start. The Universe began with a big bang, but before the "Big" bang there was a "small" existence.

So how does this help you?

No matter what your state, you are still imaging who God is because of your Spirit. From any given point, small or big, there is always the potential for growth and the potential for more. Psychology and religion is about fixing or avoiding your current condition, but the Spirit is about growing your current condition into something new and great. No matter where "small" is, the potential for growth is always present.

No one can ever say that their situation is limiting. Where there is a perceived limitation or chaos, there is always a mind - a hovering Spirit. Small is always the beginning to Big. Basically, small and big are the same thing, much in the same way as the seed being the same as the tree. All the components of the tree are contained within the seed, they are equal and one in the same. Even God chose not to start with everything, so even in our perceived smallness we are still like Him. Small does not mean we are separate or indifferent, small is just the beginning to big. The beginning to more.

The Non-Local "You" as Spirit

Your Spirit is non-local and the Spirit of God extends from and over and above the local. You are non-local, fully present, but reflected into the local. You experience events locally, but "you" are non-local. When you hear music on the radio, the music doesn't occur locally within the radio. The music exists outside of the radio and then it is reproduced locally for your experience. Nine times out of ten, a band played the actual music years ago, but the music existed over time, and then through the expanse of FM waves or AM waves, the music is set to be received through your "local" radio. Just like the music actually exists outside of the radio, you exist outside of your local presence - this is Spirit. It is here where little work is ever done. A lot of times we fight to control our circumstances or resolve situations that are local, but all we need to do is to tune our radio channel of what we want to pick up in order to pick up what we desire in life.

Play the Spirit into your situation.
Take advantage of the "you" that extends outside of you,
instead of struggling with what's in front of you.

No one can ever say that their situation is limiting, because both your Spirit and your undesired situation exist simultaneously, and both are a mirror image of God.

You have to have some guts to read the rest of this.

Yes. Everything mirrors God!

"Oohhh hell naaww! There is the devil, and he is bad, and he has all these demons screwing up my life! I can't get ahead because the devil, his demons, and his assigned people here on earth are after me to ruin my life and it's so hard! Woe is me!"

Stop looking from that perspective and look in the mirror.

2 Corinthians 3:18

But we all, with open face beholding as in a glass the glory of the Lord, are changed into the same image from glory to glory, [even] as by the Spirit of the Lord.

What's In The Mirror?

God is "small to big". God is "Chaos and Spirit", just as we are also "small to big". The Universe is "small to big", just as we are "small to big". Everything in the Universe is reflected from "small to big". A true picture of God is the state of Growth and Growing. We cannot define ourselves by our small existences or what might seem to be out of order, because that is never the finishing line, but it is always a starting point. "More" is always present because you have a mind or Spirit hovering over your chaos or your perceived limitations.

We can be excited about small or what's not working because it is still God. Spirit is always present. You are always present.

1. **Count yourself in! So whatever your current circumstance is, it is always subject to grow.**
2. **What you don't have is still a perfect picture.**
3. **You are always faced with the opportunity to create.**

I'm going to help you to digest this as we go along.

The Spirit of God hovered over the waters in the beginning, so the "waters" as stated here, represents the physical, which is your potential. Your potential never pops up into full existence at one time. Only your mind exists in fullness and has full presence, and is present. Your potential has to be shaped into something that you can enjoy, and your mind is capable of wonderful imaginations as to how things can be. Again, you are always faced with the opportunity to create, the opportunity to labor.

This is the Image of God. This is the mirror. Both what is not and what is. "What is not" is the Universe's specialty. So mirrored into you is "what is not" along with "what is", and you can always determine what will be. The problem is, is that a lot of times we chose to live in "what is not".

If God gave us everything at one time we would cease to be like Him. You and I have the same Spirit. Growing makes us just like Him. We are the Universe. We are His image. We by Spirit are omnipresent, having full presence and being fully present, but we all start with what's small. Now we have to wake up to this fact. Not waking up, leaves you in the same conditions, repeating unwanted situations over and over again.

In the Bible where the story was told about a crowd where 5000 plus people were being fed off of one boy's lunch; Jesus wasn't feeding the 5000, He was showing them how to take the little, multiply the little, and make it into more.

You have what is small, and then you have your Spirit.
You have what is without form, and then you have your Spirit.
You have what is void, and then you have your Spirit.
You have what is chaos, and then you have your Spirit.

These things; chaos, without form, void, and smallness didn't come into existence as a result of the "fall of man", but they existed from the beginning as a part of who God is. Again, there was no fall, just an event where one's eyes were open to another part of reality – what is small. The only thing that came into existence that day is that Eve evaluated herself as being less than who she really was.

This is the single most mitigating human problem, which is the source and the basis of anybody being stuck in life. What do you think of yourself?

Spirit is not just life; Spirit is also life to death and death to life. There is no point in existence where God does not exist. So we can get excited about what we don't have, because it is the stage of a Universal Creative Opportunity for Growth! But you have to get past your nakedness and shame.

Removing Fear and Shame

You shouldn't be afraid of the little, or having less. The problem enters when you move to protect the little or preserve the little that you have, or to keep it safe, and then by using your energy to keep from losing it.

Matthew 25:25

And I was afraid, and went and hid thy talent in the earth:

Every seed must die to become a tree. The entire universe works this way. From small to big. From nothing to something. From messed up to something beautiful. Even from criminal to creator. Whether you made a mess out of your life, or whether you feel that you are at a disadvantage in life, it is a canvas for creation, a canvas to be something new and better tomorrow. This is all because you have a Spirit within where nothing is an end, only beginnings. Remember, nothing is an end, not even hell.

This is who God, the Universal, the Supreme Being, and the Spirit is - something new, something greater, but always extending from what is small, what is without form and void, and even full of chaos. This is where we image God. We can take substance at any state and use our Spirit to imagine something greater and then do it. The tree and the seed are exactly the same; time brings growth with a properly understood Spirit plus properly activated labor.

The seed "messed up" and died, but after that it became an orchard.

Every baby, every seed, every business, every house, every venture, ducks, chimpanzees, alligators, space and time, is subject to the full picture of growth from small to big.

Let's go back again to Adam and Eve. In the book of **Genesis 3**, God cursed the serpent that tempted Eve, and God also cursed the ground. Notice He never cursed Adam nor Eve. It said that the Voice of God came to them walking in the garden, but the voice wasn't there to shame them, but yet Adam and Eve hid themselves from the Voice. It was within their own mind that they were ashamed of their state. This self imposed shame caused them to be afraid of the Voice. Remember you were made in God's image, the image of the Voice.

When you undervalue yourself, you are left exposed to what you think you are not. You then become afraid of your own image, the Voice. Any shame then leads to fear. You will notice that in the same chapter God said that Adam and Even became as one of Us. So again, where in this story is the "Fall" of man?

When you undervalue yourself, you are left exposed to what you think you are not. You then become afraid of your own image or sound.

You have to constantly and properly evaluate yourself, even when things seem to be "not right". You might lose substance at times, but you will never lose yourself. So, stop hiding! Listen to the Voice that is consistently walking towards you. The Voice is there to remind you that you are infinite. You are "more".

Fields of Substance

What is present before you is always great because it is still and will always be a part of who God is. Circumstances, good or bad, are always perfect for growth. But your focus should never be on the substantive existence, but on your Spirit.

All I have is $1.00. That's good!
Things are not in place. That's good!
I have less than the next person. Still good!

All that is small as it concerns you, must grow by law!

I only have a small living space. Great!
I don't have a car. Even better!
I was abused when I was a child. Great!
I was molested when I was a teenager. Even better!
I'm not loved. How wonderful!
My parents never gave me any attention. Great!
People are so unfair to me. Super!
Nobody loves me. Great!
I am all alone. Even better!

Anything that is chaos is your starting point, because you have Spirit. Your Spirit is extensive, and your Spirit is expansive!

I have HIV. Super!
I have a terminal disease. Awesome!
All of my money was lost. How powerful!
My car broke down. Great!
I am paralyzed. Thrilling!
I was raised an orphan. Superb!
I'm getting kicked out of my house. Wonderful!
My mom died of cancer. Absolutely fabulous!
My boss treats me horribly! Outstanding!

Notice! Your Spirit is still there and is still alive. The fact that you can even complain about what's wrong shows that you still have a mind or Spirit that can make assessments. Our minds can always call out a different story and reassess. Notice! No matter how horrible the situation is, the mind survives the impact enough to assess the situation. Now use that same mind to it to grow versus complaining. This is just the beginning of the true power of your Spirit.

You can choose to live on the left hand within the substances of existence which will control you, or you can choose to live on the right hand where all substances are subject to your Spirit and you can then gain control of your life and master your world!

I have been in jail for the past fifteen years. Great!
I'm a convicted felon. Greater!
I didn't graduate from high school. Super!
I'm on welfare. Absolutely marvelous!
I failed all my classes. Superb!

Your mind and Spirit are still there!

I once was a thief. How exciting!
Nobody loves me. Sensational!
I have a disease. Good!

These things make you more like God than you can ever imagine. God started there. Why doesn't God do all these great things to eliminate chaos? Well when you do them, then it is then done. This is our first peak into being just like Him. This is the first peak into the "You" that exist beyond "You" into your own Spirit.

Money, Money, Money
The Revelation on Faith and the Spirit of Life

Before we head into what's next, I would like to clue you into 4 points that you would need to know in order to live your life at an optimized state. Here are the 4:

1. **Know the truth about who you are.**
   Know your true nature, the nature of you that has absolutely no limitations.

2. **Know the truth about where you are.**
   Meaning, know the true trajectory or the place from which you operate from.

3. **Know the truth about your relationships.**
   Know the state of your relationships and connections.

4. **Know the truth about your results.**
   Take measurement of your results.
   All results are a physical picture of your spiritual world.

Keep these four things in mind as we cover the topic of money. Money is essential to all functions of life, and it is our misunderstanding of money that causes poverty in more areas than you can ever imagine.

Truth and money are essentially the same thing. Money is the basis of all exchange and truth is what we accept within our exchanges. Let's take a slightly different look at money within the light of truth. The most common discussion on money in religious circles is the concept of tithe and tithing. Let's take a closer look at tithing.

**Money is the basis of all exchange,
and truth is what we accept within our exchanges.**

Limited Belief #7

10% of your income should be given to your local religious institution as a requirement given by God. It is understood that when this is done, you should receive blessings from God based on your willingness to tithe. This is the biggest psychological trap ever perpetrated on mankind. Knowing the truth of how this is really set up is empowering to say the least.

Observation

The current understanding of tithing stems from a short passage of Scripture found in the book of Malachi. Most people address this particular passage of Scripture specifically which is found in **Malachi 3:8-10**, and this Scripture is a standard for most Western religions as it concerns members giving 10% of their income to their local church.

So let's look at the history of tithing and I think you will find what I consider to be a shocking revelation on the truth of tithing. Some say that tithing represents 10% of your income, and so here, the focus is on the percentage. The more correct way to look at tithing is one out of 10, even though it can be explained as 10%. The concept of one out of 10 can be restated as nine, then one. This is an important fact to remember.

The concept of tithe actually involves the creation of mankind, and was also instituted as a system of supply before mankind was created. Let's look at the involvement of tithe as it relates to the creation of mankind. Before mankind appeared on Earth, there existed nine orders of other created beings, which were nine orders of angels. Here the concept of nine then one becomes important, and not necessarily the idea of 10%. Mankind was positioned as the 10th order of creation after nine orders of Angels. Nine then one.

Without taking up a lot of time and space here with great detail, I'll state the simple obvious facts. Each order of Angels as it relates to capability have capabilities that are unique to them based on the order created. As you study these nine orders of angels, starting from the lowest realm to the highest realm, you will notice that the power increases and the responsibility increases as you progress through each order. Then the 10th order of beings was created to be just like God the Creator. You and I were made in God's image. The 10th order was fully made in God's image. The 10th was a representation of the whole. No angel, even Lucifer himself has the privilege of reflecting all of who God is. Nine then one.

Tithing Embedded Into Creation

The second course of tithing has a lot to do with supply. So let's look at the tithing system within nature itself. The earth within its natural settings has built within itself a system called a trophic system. As you look at the order of physical creations, you have one system that supports and supplies the next order of creation. Each part of Earth's development relative to the other parts represents only 10% of the previous system created before it. Again this is called the trophic system.

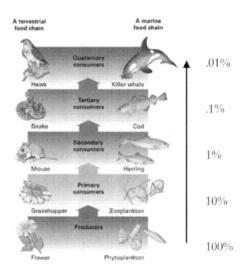

So here you find in creation that tithes is directly related to supply. This system is embedded into all of creation, so it would stand to explain or to serve as the basis as to what tithing really is. The first example of a human giving tithe is found in Genesis chapter 14 where Abraham gives a tithe to the king of Salem, Melchizedek. Notice here, that the tithe was given to an individual and not a church.

So far, we have seen three examples of tithing and none of it has anything to do with how we tithe today. The question you want to ask is, "Is tithing about building a church or is tithing about building you?" The following will help you formulate within your own mind quite clearly how this money should flow.

- Tithing is embedded into all of creation as a supply for greater systems.

- Mankind is the 10th order of creation which represents the concept of nine then one. With the one being the10th order containing within itself a reflection of the whole.

- Tithe was given initially to an individual. not a church.

Tithing is also found in the book of Leviticus chapter 27. Here you will find that sheep was passed under a rod, and every 10th sheep passed under would be considered holy unto the Lord. It was the 10th that was considered to be holy unto the Lord. Doesn't this matchup clearly with the fact that man was created as God's 10th order of beings as mankind is considered to be holy unto the Lord. Here, tithe is not considered as what is given, but to what is holy. We are a holy representation of God - this is the tithe.

As you can see so far, we have yet to find a basis of giving 10% of your income to a religious institution. Now let's look at the next example of tithing in the Bible found in the book of Deuteronomy. Deuteronomy makes one thing clear in chapter 14, that tithes was based on an increase and not income. Many of us fail to see the many lessons in the Bible that teaches us how to gain increase, and it is stated that in order to get an increase you must give tithe to your local church. In the Bible, tithe is never given to get an increase, but tithe was gathered based on increase. Increase happens first, tithe happens next. Biblically, there is no such thing as even dealing with tithes where there is debt. Holiness is about the ability to increase. You, as the tenth order of creation are designed for increase.

This is vital to understand, because man himself represents the increase of God. That is why he is the 10th order of creation. God created the nine, and then God increased Himself by creating man - 10. This is why man was commanded to be fruitful and to multiply. Tithing is not to get increase. You are the tithe, a representation increase. That's why it was states in Leviticus, nine then one. Each day of creation represented an increase, and the previous creation supported and supplied the next creation. The next creation was an increase in every way, but the increase was supported by the previous level of creation.

The next thing you want to notice in **Deuteronomy 14** is that not only was the tithe a support for the Levite and the stranger, but as it clearly says **in Deuteronomy 14:24-25**, the tithe was for the consumption of the individual who had brought the tithe. Again, you must adamantly remember that tithe is about supply.

- No one tithed unless they had enough. **Leviticus 27**

- Tithe was paid on increase and not income. **Deuteronomy 14**

- Tithe was specifically used for consumption of the one who was tithing.

Let's take a closer look at the main Scripture used as a support for tithing to a local church.

Malachi 3:8-11

8 Will a man rob God? Yet ye have robbed me. But ye say, Wherein have we robbed thee? In tithes and offerings.

9 Ye are cursed with a curse: for ye have robbed me, even this whole nation.

10 Bring ye all the tithes into the storehouse, that there may be meat in mine house, and prove me now herewith, saith the LORD of hosts, if I will not open you the windows of heaven, and pour you out a blessing, that there shall not be room enough to receive it.

11 And I will rebuke the devourer for your sakes, and he shall not destroy the fruits of your ground; neither shall your vine cast her fruit before the time in the field, saith the LORD of hosts.

Here, as most would consider, tithing is associated with robbing God if it is not paid. This is a gross misunderstanding of the Scripture because the Scripture is not given in its entirety. Most people fail to realize this. Most people are told that if they don't pay a tithe, that they will be cursed by God. Well, since it is there, I will add a verse that turns this whole notion topsy-turvy.

Malachi 3:7

Even from the days of your fathers ye are gone away from mine ordinances, and have not kept [them]. Return unto me, and I will return unto you, saith the LORD of hosts. But ye said, Wherein shall we return?

Notice this Scripture, which is one verse above what most consider as the tithing main scripture in the Bible Malachi 3:8-10. Notice how verse seven is not used as a starting point, but verse eight is used as a starting point. Notice in verse seven, God is asking for man to physically return unto Him. So tithing is about you and I coming back or returning back to God and is not based on paying God any type of money. So then the question is asked, how do we do this? How do we return?

Following verse seven, you then go into verse eight. See how this changes everything. We rob God by not presenting ourselves back to Him, by not returning to Him. This one statement is crucial to all economics. This one statement is crucial to the value of money and how money should work in your life. This one statement is crucial to the bases of all exchange. We rob God by not reflecting who He is in the Earth, as His "tenth order" is designed to represent the fullness of God in the physical. To reflect God is to return to Him. Now to fully understand this, you must read the whole book of Malachi and not just three or four versus in chapter 3. When you depart from God's design for you, you lose the ability to increase. So you must return.

What is a true offering? Our true offering is about how we choose to reflect God on Earth (manifestation). As the earth unfolds, it unfolds in portions of tenths. That's why tithing is about increase and not income. We are taught to use our income to get to God or prove ourselves to God, when God simply asks us to return to Him (reflection) so we can increase in this life on Earth.

How does this help you?

Let's start in Psalms 100 where there is a verse that states that you must enter into His gates with Thanksgiving, and then into His courts with Praise. Within this scripture there is a standard for a solid foundation when it comes to financial success. By doing a short word history, you will be clued into the ingenious pattern located within the concept of Thanksgiving.

Psalms 100:4

Enter into his gates with thanksgiving, [and] into his courts with praise: be thankful unto him, [and] bless his name.

Most of today's modern churches and mega-ministries have adopted a format of services termed as Praise and Worship, and rightfully so. But there is a component that is identified in **Psalms 100** that precedes Praise and Worship, and that is the component of Thanksgiving. Thanksgiving is financial in nature. Here Thanksgiving is a procedure ordered by God in the book of Nehemiah chapter 10, when God was having Israel to put in order what was being brought to the Sanctuary concerning their personal goods. Again, you must think of tithes in terms of supply and increase as it is stated in the Bible and not as a unit of income given to a local ministry. This will help you to understand the full implication of the real meaning of tithes.

To get to the bottom line, tithing is about self-value or the personal price you put on yourself. All financial success starts with your own personal evaluation, and tithe is how you order or perceive your own value. The word "thank" is derived from the word "think". Both carry the same basic meaning and extend from the same word etymology. Thanksgiving is all about what you think, and what you think about carries value. What you think becomes your actual value which unfolds out into the rest of your life.

*For as he thinketh in heart, so is he...***Proverbs 23.7**

So let's take a closer look at the relationship between these words, and as we do this, there is another word that is derived from this same process which is "appreciation", which means to grow in value.

- **Thought**

Your thoughts are the basis of all value. Nothing exist without a thought proceeding it. This lends itself to the notion that every thought is omnipresent because thoughts precede things.

- **Think**

Thinking is your open template to organize your desires, set destinations, and reflect on presentations presented to you. Thinking is the process used to flow your thoughts out in preparation for the transformation of those same thoughts to grow into physical reality.

- **Thank**

The word thank is associated with gratitude, but it is also a direct derivative of the word think. They are primarily the same word. What you think is associated with gratitude. Responsible thinking is done with gratitude.

- **Appreciation**

Appreciation is also associated with gratitude and thankfulness, but appreciation is also the basis of value, which means to gain in value. So value and worth are closely knitted into what you think. Your thoughts should always grow in value.

So to Enter His gates with Thanksgiving...means to order your thoughts so you can grow in value. This happens before you enter His gates with praise.

Now, let's ask some tough questions about thoughts and thinking. What do people think about? Thoughts can generally be broken down into two subcategories:

What You See (Sensory or Responsive Thinking)

What You Want (Developmental Thinking)

That's it. There's nothing else to think about. I want you to meditate on this for a little bit. What do people think about? If anyone was to define the content of thought or thinking, only these two modes of thinking can come up. Generally, nothing else enters the mind of thought. Thoughts are amazing, but they only flow in two directions. You are either responding to life or you are creating life. The first objective of personal pricing or placing a value on yourself is taking measurement of the direction of your thoughts. This is the basic rudiment of tithing, to order your thoughts just like Israel had to order their possessions in **Nehemiah 10**. Your thoughts are:

Reactionary   or   **Creative**

You are either responding to life or you are creating life.

Your actions then become the point of value as it follows one of the two modes of thinking. It is here where you determine your value. Your personal value is found in your mode of thinking, and then your subsequent actions qualify and quantify what is thought of.

What has more value? Following something or someone that exist already, or creating something new? Your value extends from what you think and who you are that is related to what's new and what's next. This is then immediately reflected into your personal economy. Poverty never starts at the point where money is lacking. Poverty and wealth starts with your ability to order your thoughts which then unfold into things. This is a true and exact definition of tithing. Tithing is returning your thought process back to God. Do not ever devalue the importance of things.

The Importance of Things - Revelation On Faith

Hebrews 11:1

Now faith is the substance of things hoped for, the evidence of things not seen.

It is clearly stated here that Faith is the Substance. The Substance of Things. Faith is also the Evidence of Things... Without "things" there is no Faith. Things come from what you think. Your Faith is associated with the quality of your thinking. Thoughts turn into things.

Hebrews 11:6

But without faith [it is] impossible to please [him]: for he that cometh to God....

STOP!!!!

Hebrews 11:6...For he that cometh to God...

Malachi 3:7...Return unto me...

Herein is the issue of tithing...Returning to God...Without Faith it is impossible to please God...Faith is the Substance... Proximity to the knowledge of who you truly are produces things.

Faith is taking what you think (things not seen) and bringing it into what can be experienced as Substance (what can be seen). Then the rest of **Hebrews 11** talks about people who were able to make things happen based on the quality of their thoughts and not their surrounding circumstances. God spent the entire creation process bringing Things from the unseen into that which can be seen. Then God created you and I in His own image and said do the same thing, be fruitful and multiply.

True success is about substance. True spirituality is about substance. We want to in today's religion make our experience with God "spiritual" and in many cases this is done at the sacrifice of having substance – it is generally said, "To be without is spiritual". God is not a brain activity! God is I AM once you become. People are generally afraid to become anything because they are taught to deny earthly things to obtain a spiritual bliss.

God is I AM once you become.

God created "things" in six days then rested on the seventh day. What we generally try to do is find peace or rest without Substance. Rest does not come without tithe, which is to return to God and produce from the place and space where God exist versus trying to produce and make things happen from your own place and space.

Monuments

I want to refer to things here as monuments. Monuments are things that are a result of your thinking. So your monuments or better stated, (money- mints), the "money that you mint" are staple to your ability to rest and be at peace. No, this is no joke. The root of the word monument comes from the Latin word "monere", which means to remind. Again, you can only re-mind if you have the evidence that can bring something back to the mind. The root word for money is "moneta" which means to mint is a derivative of "monere", which is the same as monument. Stay with me. To think, mind, mint, money, and monument all come from the same root word.

Without "things" there is no rest.
Without "monuments" there is no peace.

The prefix to all of these words is "mon-" which means the mind or to think. This is why I said, it is so important to value what you think. It is also imperative to think only thoughts that have value. As the old adage states, "A mind is a terrible thing to waste", so stop wasting your mind. Literally, wasting your mind is wasting money. Every thought that you have subtly extends the expanse of the universe. Your very thoughts extend beyond you without limitation. If you equate your thoughts with who you are, then you are also without limitation. Your body, your surroundings, and its systems of memory which includes your brain are just a local representation of your thoughts which exist everywhere at one time. Consider your immediate and local presence in the world as an opportunity to convey a vast amount of your thoughts which exist in heaven to be converted into a physical reality that comes from you for mankind to experience and for you to enjoy. To begin this exercise I'm going to give you a series of word associations. But the main word of focus here is "appreciation".

With the notion that thoughts grow in value, it should be readily understood that your very existence, your life, and what you do in life should always be set to grow in value. You and I are designed to grow exponentially. Growth is closely associated to your capacity to think and to garner the awareness of your potential to contribute to life. Therefore, in order for you to have a great life, you have to place a premium value on what you think. You have to hold yourself to this value that you set for yourself, and you must also hold others to the same standard towards yourself. People must see your worth, and your worth starts with your thoughts which are knowledge.

This is Entering into His gates with Thanksgiving...

The Point of Nehemiah and Malachi

So God asked Israel to bring all the tithes into the storehouse. Now you must remember according to Deuteronomy 14 that the tithes was consumed by the one who brought the tithes and was also shared with the temple servants including the Levites, gate porters, singers and musicians.

Tithing is about ordering, ordering your thoughts for future production. In the book of Nehemiah, God had the people to order their tithes and offerings into thirds and tenths. All this was done before they entered the Sanctuary. You enter into His gates with Thanksgiving. This is Substance being put into order, or ordering what you think; and your thinking is a substance that is not seen. This is the basis of Faith. Ordering what you think is a vital process as it concerns your ability to produce anything What you want in life.

If there is disorder in your thinking,
there will be no order in your producing.

I consistently state that your economy does not start with the cash that you have on hand, your economy starts with how you order your thoughts. The book of Malachi is a reference to the book Nehemiah. So if the tithe and offering scripture was a literal template as to what you should bring to a church, then you would seriously come up short if all you brought was 10% of your income. You would also be required to bring your first fruits, a third of a shekel of gold or silver, and your first born child. Pastors would be really rolling then. They would have 10% of your income, along with having your gold and silver, your food and your children. **Nehemiah 10:32-39**

Your younger children would be asking, "where's my big brother?".

And you would have to say, "the Bible said I had to give him to the church".

The baby would scream, "Mommy! The Kellog's CoCo Puffs are gone!"

You have to respond, "No, Pastor Dan has your CoCo Puffs. We had to bring him the first of our groceries also".

All this would have to be added to your ten percent if that's the point that God was making.

Nehemiah and Malachi was about solving a very serious problem. The people's minds had wondered away from God, and because of it, they ended up in a state of destitution. Their city walls were torn down and they were subject to the economy of other nations. They suffered a deep depression because they no longer had an economic foundation of their own. All trade had stopped and they were living in an impoverished condition. Their storehouse had literally become hotel rooms for their enemies. The Ammonites and Moabites had relocated within the core of their economy, and so the state of their economy was being continuously drained by others. The opposite of right thinking is having your vibrancy drained by others. This directly affects your ability to produce.

If you study Malachi 1 and 2, God was fussing at Israel because their thinking was totally backwards, and because of their state of mind they would always respond to God with a dumb question, therefore in **Malachi 3:7**, God was asking them to return to Him. They asked how. Then God gave them an economic solution to their backwards thinking. This was the point of tithe - to enter into His gates with Thanksgiving. Without right thinking there cannot be right production.

So we see the production of God at the beginning of time was ordered into segments of tenths as we discussed earlier, and then we see the order and structure of reality set into thirds - the heavens unseen, the heavens seen, and then the earth. Then you have 2/3 of angels set to manage heaven and 1/3 of angels that was cast out of heaven with Lucifer to manage things that don't work. Christ is then the first born.

The same breakdown was established in **Nehemiah 10** because God was leading them back to an understanding of something greater. The book of Nehemiah starts with the books of Moses being read to the children of Israel. From this reading, they had come to the realization, as their history was read to them, that they were a great people. Israel had to be re-minded.

This leads us to the first point that I stated at the beginning of this chapter.

1.   Know the truth about who you are.

Know your true nature, the nature of you that has absolutely no limitations.

Know Who You Are

Without the knowledge of who you are, you are left at the mercy of unseen forces. This is the lower third of the angelic realm. When you take control over this third and the tenth, you have control over the whole. Anytime you don't think for yourself to create results, results are created for you anyway by outside entities that do not work for your best interest.

Thinking has within it real properties of production. That's why your thinking has to be valued, because it is your thinking that creates value. Again, if you do not order your thinking, you will have disorder in your life. So the third given back to God represents turning over the power that has been subject to the lower third of Angels, and turn it back to following your ability to think and produce for yourself.

The devil and his angels are not entities that are set and designed to come against you and your success, but they are simply entities created by God to manage what you don't care to think about, or your inability to think correctly. This lower third of angelic host, heading by Lucifer are called ground workers. This is represented by the third of a shekel found in **Nehemiah 10.** You are created to order this third of the energy spectrum, but if you do not take the time to think constructively, you follow the order of the third versus ordering and commanding the third that is really subject to you.

Every last thought that you have is creative. Every last thought produces something. When you think outside of what God has called on your life, for example, when you think lower of yourself, God's two thirds of Angels cannot manage, nor are they designed to manage your mess. Let me put it this way, when you think the worst, you have a host of angels which are a third of the angelic hosts that you just hired to help you with your negative thoughts.

God has designed a way to bring this third of existence back to Him. To think the thoughts of God as it concerns yourself is entering into His gates with Thanksgiving. You return unto Him...

Philippians 2:5-6

5 Let this mind be in you, which was also in Christ Jesus:

6 Who, being in the form of God, thought it not robbery to be equal with God:

As you see here, we are made in the image of God and should not think it robbery to be equal to God.

Malachi 3:8

Will a man rob God? Yet ye have robbed me. But ye say, Wherein have we robbed thee? In tithes and offerings

So where do we rob God? We rob God in our inability to think and order things within our minds so that they can appear into physical reality for our own experience and enjoyment, and then the experience and enjoyment of others.

1 Timothy 4:14-15

14 Neglect not the gift that is in thee, which was given thee by prophecy, with the laying on of the hands of the presbytery.

15 Meditate upon these things; give thyself wholly to them; that thy profiting may appear to all.

When the serpent spoke to Eve in the beginning, Eve lost consciousness of herself. She was easily convinced that she was not like God, and felt she had to partake of the fruit in order to know the things of God. She had failed to realize in that moment that she was created in

God's image. So the cast-down-third now took precedence and Eve was now subject to things outside of her desire. Being subject to anything outside of what you want in life, is living in death. This was the same state that the people in Nehemiah found themselves in and needed to correct it by returning this lower third and the tenth that they had given up power over back to God.

The "third" here actually represents your emotions psychological-ly. But that's another book. Give your earthly response system back to God. Your emotions are the lower third of your existence. This lower third is the same ground that God cursed in Genesis chapter 2. "Cursed is the ground for thy sake", God said. Instead of the ground working you, you work the ground. Instead of your emotions working you, you work your emotions. Instead of money working you, you work your money. God put all things under your feet. Again, that's another book.

As I said earlier in terms of thinking:

You are either responding to life or you are creating life.

All of this affects your financial bottom line. So where is the 10th or tithe in all of this? Here is how you order your thinking...

The Tenth and Birthing

Here, I want to focus on the concept of tithing as viewed from the standpoint of 9 then 1 as found in *Leviticus 27*. We find this exact pattern as it relates to birth within the incubation period of a human being after conception. An embryo develops within the mother's womb for a period of nine months and is birthed in the tenth month. This remains consistent as humans model the theme of tithing within their personal make-up. So after nine months of incubation or development, then birth takes place.

Or better yet,

Conception, then **9**  **1**

Birthing and development is also a word concept that shows up in the first chapter of Genesis where most people think creation took place. As stated earlier, I consider creation to have happened at one moment in time, and out of that initial substance, everything else was developed and birthed, hence the process of expansion through birthing. From day one, God divided things out of what was already in existence.

Genesis 1:4

*And God saw the light, that [it was] good: and God **divided** the light from the darkness.*

Genesis 1:6

*And God said, Let there be a firmament in the midst of the waters, and let it **divide** the waters from the waters.*

Genesis 1:7

*And God made the firmament, and **divided** the waters which [were] under the firmament from the waters which [were] above the firmament: and it was so.*

Genesis 1:14

*And God said, Let there be lights in the firmament of the heaven to **divide** the day from the night; and let them be for signs, and for seasons, and for days, and years:*

Genesis 1:18

*And to rule over the day and over the night, and to **divide** the light from the darkness: and God saw that [it was] good.*

Genesis 1:11

And God said, Let the earth bring forth grass, the herb **yielding** *seed, [and] the fruit tree* **yielding** *fruit after his kind, whose seed [is] in itself, upon the earth: and it was so.*

Genesis 1:12

And the earth brought forth grass, [and] herb **yielding** *seed after his kind, and the tree* **yielding** *fruit, whose seed [was] in itself, after his kind: and God saw that [it was] good.*

From these early scriptures you see an extreme process of dividing and yielding. I believe that the study of substance is the study of our Faith. It is a way of knowing God-processes. Within nature we find the continuous wonders of the mind of God. Nothing in nature is by accident. Everything is by design, and this very design serves as a template to our soul's make-up and the nature of our own existence. You do not have to find a church to find out who God is, just split open an atom or a molecule and it will tell you who God is.

As time passed in the beginning, God took what was, and then through His own system of Sound, He pushed new things into existence. It is very important that you grasp what is being stated here, because it serves as a basis for truly understanding how you can attain anything you want in life.

You must also understand that you can be facing an old understanding as to how life works and must allow some mental space to digest a more correct order of things. So I would like to post a couple of reminders for you before I proceed with the next part:

1. You are made in God's Image. So technically you are not made, but reflected as an Image.

2. God did not condemn man, but man opened himself to the consequences of being subject to a lower mind set or diminished thinking. But the gift of God is...

Romans 6:23

For the wages of sin [is] death; but the gift of God [is] eternal life through Jesus Christ our Lord.

Death is a result and not a condemnation. This in no way constitutes a change in what God's commandment is concerning you. But, the gift of God is... some people get so caught up in the "wages of sin" that they forget "But the gift of God is...".

Ephesians 1:3-5

³ Blessed be the God and Father of our Lord Jesus Christ, who hath blessed us with all spiritual blessings in heavenly places in Christ:

⁴ According as he hath chosen us in him before the foundation of the world, that we should be holy and without blame before him in love:

⁵ Having predestinated us unto the adoption of children by Jesus Christ to himself, according to the good pleasure of his will,

This is God's promise towards you and I, and it cannot change because God does not change. Your "sin" does not change God.

Hebrew 6:17-18

¹⁷ Wherein God, willing more abundantly to shew unto the heirs of promise the immutability of his counsel, confirmed it by an oath:

¹⁸ That by two immutable things, in which it was impossible for God to lie, we might have a strong consolation, who have fled for refuge to lay hold upon the hope set before us:

James 1:17-18

17 Every good gift and every perfect gift is from above, and cometh down from the Father of lights, with whom is no variableness, neither shadow of turning.

18 Of his own will begat he us with the word of truth, that we should be a kind of firstfruits of his creatures.

So as you can clearly see here, you are a kind of first fruit/tithes which is of His own will. Now check this out in Ephesians.

Ephesians 1:11-12

11 In whom also we have obtained an inheritance, being predestinated according to the purpose of him who worketh all things after the counsel of his own will:

12 That we should be to the praise of his glory, who first trusted in Christ.

God trusted Christ based on what Christ had to say about you.

Ephesians 1:13-14

13 In whom ye also trusted, after that ye heard the word of truth, the gospel of your salvation: in whom also after that ye believed, ye were sealed with that holy Spirit of promise,

14 Which is the earnest of our inheritance until the redemption of the purchased possession, unto the praise of his glory.

Now you have to trust what Christ says about you...

Jude 1:24

Now unto him that is able to keep you from falling, and to present [you] faultless before the presence of his glory with exceeding joy,

The story about you coming from the mouth of Christ towards God does not change! You can be ignorant of it and live in death, or you can awake to it and have life to swallow up death. More about Christ's Word towards you later. But I will start here.

John 1:1-4

¹In the beginning was the Word, and the Word was with God, and the Word was God.

²The same was in the beginning with God.

³All things were made by him; and without him was not any thing made that was made.

⁴In him was life; and the life was the light of men.

3. Death is not a sentence. Death is a state of being. God said "thou shall surely die", God did not say, "and I will kill you".

Genesis 2:17

But of the tree of the knowledge of good and evil, thou shalt not eat of it: for in the day that thou eatest thereof thou shalt surely die.

Death is a choice based on how you view yourself, your life, and then your subsequent actions based on your thinking. Death is not used as a blanket sentence imposed by God on all of mankind. The "wages" of sin (missing the mark) is death. Death as in "living in a state of death", not as in "I will kill you" type of death. Death is tied to your actions which is based off of your "thoughts", and is not tied into what God does as a punishment. Death is not a punishment, Death is a wage!!! Death is a monetary consideration that set's your state of being. Those who make little, have little. Those who make much, have much.

Financial issues stem from death. So churchin' doesn't solve your financial problems, neither does tithing to a particular church solves your financial problems. In order to solve personal problems and more importantly, to solve your financial problems, you must deal with the subject of death and what extends out of your personal death that controls your life.

Those with valued thoughts or tithe towards their life, live in life. Those who have a devalued evaluation of themselves, live in death, just as Eve devalued herself. This is the express reason why both Adam and Eve hid themselves when they heard the Voice of God walking towards them in Genesis 3.

Tithe Patterns and True Money Patterns

So, let's compare and break down three tithe patterns that are closely related:

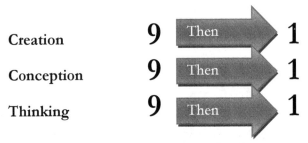

Creation   9 Then 1

Conception   9 Then 1

Thinking   9 Then 1

Remember that nine represents development. One represents what is birthed or tithe.

Creation - How the Earth Works.

Creation   9 Then 1

As I said earlier, substances within the earth are continually pushed incrementally towards newer and greater stages by the Voice of God. Remember, this is the same Voice that was walking in the garden towards Adam and Eve. As the Voice spoke, it resulted in a trophic system that rates at ten percent of the previous phase of development at each stage or increment of time as it concerns energy and supply.

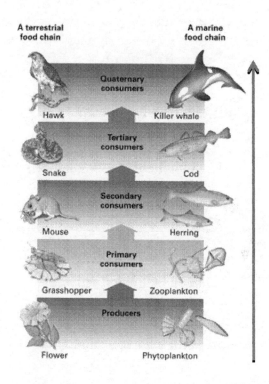

If you were to use a more detailed chart of Earth's development, you will be able to see an order of unfolding that takes place. You must also understand that all life unfolds. If you ever looked closely at a rose, its growth process involves unfolding. Everything that is in its earlier stages of life unfolds into greater life. Even a fertilized egg unfolds into an embryo, and the embryo continues to unfold into a fully functional body. After seeds germinate and pierce the soil, you can literally witness the unfolding of the plants and trees.

When you are trying to accomplish anything in life, you can look at it from this same standpoint. Every idea that you have within your mind is set to unfold. We generally spend a lot of time trying to make things happen. The correct process is to set things in its optimal state to start and then allow it to unfold. This is where you have to place a heightened value on what you think, because all thinking is set to unfold.

When you are experiencing a series of bad results or negative events in your life, you are simply witnessing an unfolding of something. That unfolding has a source or a beginning point, and that source is always within you. What unfolds becomes a witness to what is on your mind whether it is conscious or unconscious. This is why it needs to be made clear that you have to order your thinking which is the true meaning of tithe and tithing. Enter His gates with Thanks...Think...Money...

**True finances start with what you think,
and your thinking always unfolds into experience.**

So the process of development is really about unfolding, and life will continue to unfold whether you make plans are not. As life is always set to unfold, it is with the mind and what you think that determines what is contained in the folds of life. What's unique about unfolding is that if something unfolds from within itself, it is unfolding from its own identity. What is also important to note here is that supply is always built for the next sounding of God. God's Word does not exist without supply. As life unfolds, and as things unfold, it always unfolds after its kind.

Genesis 1:11-12

*And God said, Let the earth bring forth grass, the herb yielding seed, [and] the fruit tree yielding fruit **after his kind**, whose seed [is] in itself, upon the earth: and it was so. And the earth brought forth grass, [and] herb yielding seed **after his kind**, and the tree yielding fruit, whose seed [was] in itself, **after his kind**: and God saw that [it was] good.*

Genesis 1:21

*And God created great whales, and every living creature that moveth, which the waters brought forth abundantly, **after their kind**, and every winged fowl **after his kind**: and God saw that [it was] good.*

Genesis 1:24-25

*And God said, Let the earth bring forth the living creature **after his kind**, cattle, and creeping thing, and beast of the earth **after his kind**: and it was so. And God made the beast of the earth **after his kind**, and cattle **after their kind**, and everything that creepeth upon the earth **after his kind**: and God saw that [it was] good.*

So not only do you see a process of dividing and birthing, you see development and you see things being produced after its kind. When something comes from something, it is a reflection of what it came from - an Image. All of this is embedded in the processes of who God is, and everything is moved forward into greater existences by His Voice or Sound.

John 1:1

In the beginning was the Word, and the Word was with God, and the Word was God.

This was the same Voice walking in the garden. This Voice walked with the Image of who Adam and Eve were, but they hid themselves from their own image. Please note here the association of the image with the voice.

Your Image = The Voice

Your Reflected Image = The Sound of God

You = The Word of God

Along with the created order of substances, each producing after its kind, there was a created order of beings.

1   **Seraphim**
2   **Cherubim**
3   **Thrones**
4   **Dominions**
5   **Virtues**
6   **Powers**
7   **Principalities**
8   **Archangels**
9   **Angels**

Then man, **10**!

You are a tithe presented back to God. It's important to get this concept deep down into your spirit and your consciousness in order for you to know your true value. God, just as in the order of the nature that He developed, produced an Image after his own likeness and this image comes with a full supply of substance. This is not religious rhetoric, but the state of reality in which how life works as God commanded it to be so. This has not changed since the beginning of time, but our minds can be blind to this fact. Look at the next concept of nine then one.

Human Development

Conception

When a child is conceived, it goes through nine months of development and then begins to live outside of the womb generally within the 10th month. What I want to note here is while a child is being developed within the womb of the mother, the child is resting in water. Let's look at this next set of scriptures to find out why this is important.

Psalms 139:13-14

13 For thou hast possessed my reins: thou hast covered me in my mother's womb.

14 I will praise thee; for I am fearfully and wonderfully made: marvellous are thy works; and that my soul knoweth right well.

The question is asked in Psalms 139:7,

Psalms 139:7

Whither shall I go from thy spirit? or whither shall I flee from thy presence?

David is saying here in **Psalms 139:13**, that thou hast covered me in my mother's womb. Here, David is referring to the Spirit of God in verse seven. Now let's look at this first in Genesis.

Genesis 1:2

And the earth was without form, and void; and darkness [was] upon the face of the deep. And the Spirit of God moved upon the face of the waters.

The word "moved" here denotes that the Spirit hovered over the face of the waters, and as we see in Psalms, the Spirit covered David in his mother's womb which is filled with water. Is this a coincidence? I don't think so. From this, a process of development takes place over nine months. Starting with the process of divisions just like in Genesis...

Your Life Unfolding

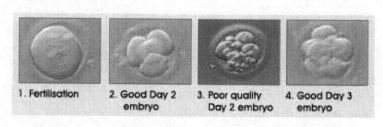

1. Fertilisation   2. Good Day 2 embryo   3. Poor quality Day 2 embryo   4. Good Day 3 embryo

Divisions then development...We see the exact same process in Genesis chapter one with the development of the Earth. Look closely at this next graphic:

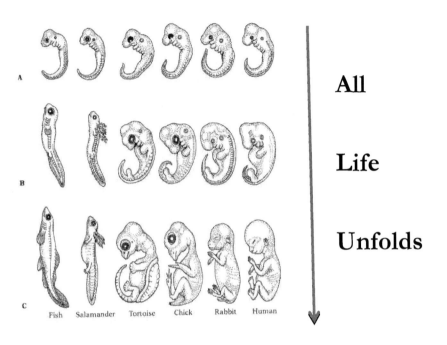

All

Life

Unfolds

A

B

C

Fish   Salamander   Tortoise   Chick   Rabbit   Human

Every creation in the trophic system basically starts off with the similar type of embryo but ends up at a different point of finality. These different points of finality are based on the Sound or the Word of God. All of your points of finality that are success oriented is completed already by your thoughts, now it only has to unfold.

Psalms 139:15-18

[15] *My substance was not hid from thee, when I was made in secret, and curiously wrought in the lowest parts of the earth.*

[16] *Thine eyes did see my substance, yet being unperfect; and in thy book all my members were written, which in continuance were fashioned, when as yet there was none of them.*

[17] How precious also are thy thoughts unto me, O God! how great is the sum of them!

[18] If I should count them, they are more in number than the sand: when I awake, I am still with thee.

In verse 16, the word "book" is used here, but not in the sense of how we understand a book to be. This is not a book with pages or a biblical like scroll that's seen in the movies. The history of the word "book" that shows up here is more in line with a narrative, or to narrate. It means to speak in line or speak in a specific order with the connotation of counting while inscribing through speaking. This "book" is a vocal act of God. As God narrates a description of Himself, an inscription of you is carved into existence. When Moses asked of God, "What is thy name?", God responded, "I Am that I Am" - **Exodus 3:13, 14**. God's name is who you and I decide to be. This all starts with your thinking.

The Bible says in the first part of Colossians that your life is hid with Christ in God. It also states that you were chosen in God before the foundation of the world **(Ephesians 1),** and that you were are fearfully and wonderfully made. In **Psalms 139** it says that His thoughts are precious towards you and that your members were listed in His book and all your members in continuance were fashioned.

Psalms 139:16 starts off with, "Thine eyes did see my Substance"...substance here means folded or to fold together. So the intent here, just as the rest of creation proves, is to unfold. But the unfolding is not arbitrary. The unfolding happens according to the book, and according to God's utterance which is a narrative in the sense of counting. You have to trust your unfolding and not allow your mind to rethink your future based off of environmental concerns.

Psalms 138:8

The LORD will perfect [that which] concerneth me: thy mercy, O LORD, [endureth] for ever: forsake not the works of thine own hands.

And so this work "on you" extends out into the future forever. I have to apologize for those who believe that God's work ends at what they might call "hell". I didn't mean to ruin your religion. Yes I did. Listen to this...

1 Corinthians 3:13

Every man's work shall be made manifest: for the day shall declare it, because it shall be revealed by fire; and the fire shall try every man's work of what sort it is.

To try a man's work, not to punish man. Let's continue...

1 Corinthians 3:15

If any man's work shall be burned, he shall suffer loss: but he himself shall be saved; yet so as by fire.

Limited Belief #8

Hell was designed to punish man once he dies if his work wasn't up to par or if he died in his sin. The concept of hell originated in the long held belief that man had the power to secure some type of order in his afterlife. This influence stemmed from thousands of years of Egyptian practices and has found its way into modern Biblical interpretations. Hell as taught by Jesus was a literal location on the outskirts of the city walls that was used to discard and burn trash. It was used as a perfect allegory to describe our current conditions when one psychologically distances oneself from the truth that makes one free. It is not, nor is it explained in the Bible as an afterlife existence.

Observation

Many preachers have preached for many years the theology of hell, fire and brimstone. The gnashing of teeth. None of these preachers have been to hell and brought back an actual report, but they seem to know a lot about it.

First we have to start with a simple fact that every Old Testament reference to hell represented a current state or a current condition. It never represented an afterlife existence. Its definition means pit or grave. Weirdly enough, it is derived from the same Hebrew word that means to ask, or to ask for. Hell literally means to be in limbo (this is where the Catholics draw the idea of purgatory). It also means a hollow place. So how is it figured that hell is an afterlife existence and it comes from the Word of God?

As we refer back to the book of Malachi where we pick up the tithe story, there were a series of questions asked by the people as God exposed them to the state that they were in. All these questions came from a hollow place. When you find yourself broke, disgusted, and it seems as though the people who are against you are winning, nobody is concerned about your well-being, nothing is falling into place, there is a sense of brokenness and heartbreak. This is Hell!!! This is the fire. What is asked in every case, "Why am I here? Why am I in this state?". It is an asking that comes from a hollow place.

The current concept of hell was meted out by a bunch of imma-ture and amateur theologians looking for a place to park their dark piousness. It's sad to say, so many Christians have bought into it.

In the New Testament, hell refers to a steep valley area where trash and dead animals were burned. Would it be a stretch to think and to know that any reference to hell as it relates to a place where humans to go would be an allegory or a parable as to how life works in the here and now? Did not Jesus use parables or parallels to teach much of what He wanted to get across? Why then all of a sudden did "hell" have to become a place that actually exists? How spiritually elementary of some folks.

1 Corinthians 15:54-55

54 So when this corruptible shall have put on incorruption, and this mortal shall have put on immortality, then shall be brought to pass the saying that is written, Death is swallowed up in victory.

55 O death, where is thy sting? O grave, where is thy victory?

So now I am left to answer the question of what happens after death? I can answer that with a convincing line of scriptures, but the point of this book is not for that. A shortcut to the answer to that question is to ask a more appropriate question, and with that, this question is also the answer to what happens after death:

What happens after life? Answer that, and you will have the answer to both questions.

How does this helps you?

The idea of there being a point in which God can lose you destroys your ability to think to the extent of what it takes for successful living. Many do not know that the concept of hell was taught as a slave tactic to ruin the minds of the Christian slaves. Punishment had to be an active part in subjecting the consciousness of the African in America to the mental stronghold of a slave master. How else do you think one white person could command the obedience of 30 to 40 slaves that was clearly more powerful physically? They had to command the mind through twisted religious beliefs.

The scriptures on hell became a powerful tool as the African was convinced that he or she had to do all within their power to protect their afterlife. Historically, Africans carried a strong tradition in preserving the afterlife, so the Biblical reference to hell became a perfect tool as it was the Christian thing to do when it came to obeying their Master. But the concept of hell then became woven into modern Christian philosophy without foundation, but people just believed it because that's what the pastor read and said.

The Africans in America became more diminished in their own capacity to think. You must understand that your personal belief system will unfold out into your state of life. To carry within your mind the idea that God can and will someday destroy you is psychologically and physiologically debilitating to your present conditions and to your ability to know that God is committed to your successful existence forever.

Hebrews 13:5-6

⁵ Let your conversation be without covetousness; and be content with such things as ye have: for He hath said, **_I will never leave thee, nor forsake thee._**

⁶ So that we may boldly say, The Lord is my helper, and I will not fear what man shall do unto me.

Matthew 28:20

Teaching them to observe all things whatsoever I have commanded you: and, **_lo, I am with you alway, [even] unto the end of the world. Amen_**

Romans 8:38-39

For I am persuaded, that neither death, nor life, nor angels, nor principalities, nor powers, nor things present, nor things to come, Nor height, nor depth, nor any other creature, **_(nothing) shall be able to separate us from the love of God, which is in Christ Jesus our Lord._**

John 17:12

*While I was with them in the world, I kept them in thy name**: those that thou gavest me I have kept, and none of them is lost,** but the son of perdition; that the scripture might be fulfilled.*

Colossians 3:3

For ye are dead, and **_your life is hid with Christ in God._**

1 Corinthians 3:15

If any man's work shall be burned, he shall suffer loss: **_but he himself shall be saved;_** *yet so as by fire.*

My mom used to say at times, "I'm going to kill you!", but I never walked around the house waiting to die. So why do we walk around with a state of mind "waiting to die", waiting to be judged as some will go

to heaven and some will be sentenced to hell? This same story is appro-
bated by the story Santa Clause where we are taught the fear of loss:

> You better watch out
> You better not cry
> Better not pout
> I'm telling you why
> Santa Claus is coming to town
> He's making a list
> And checking it twice;
> Gonna find out Who's naughty and nice
> Santa Claus is coming to town
> He sees you when you're sleeping
> He knows when you're awake
> He knows if you've been bad or good
> So be good for goodness sake!

The concept of hell is an unhealthy mindset when it comes to
basic thought formulation, because you then carry the potential thought
that at some point God can and will lose you permanently. This warps
the understanding of God's true purpose of reflecting Himself into the
reality of the seen world and threatens the outlook of our truest potential.

Ephesians 1:4, God chose you and I before the foundation
world. He chose us early, so choosing us (judgment) in the end is a non-
factor. We are already chosen and God does not change His mind. If
you read Ephesians 1 carefully and in context, God did the choosing in
the beginning so we would be without blame during the course of our
life.

According to **Jude 1:24**, Christ presents you and I faultless before
the throne of God and He keeps us from a fallen status. Using just these
two scripture references, it is impossible to condemn people to hell, if we
were created to the praise of His glory. Don't let the ideas about hell
interrupt your ability to think.

Developmental Thinking

Thinking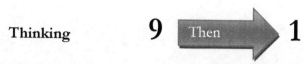

Now we are looking at the concept of entering into His gates with Thanksgiving. Let's look a little closer at some of the concepts we have looked at earlier and begin to put this puzzle together.

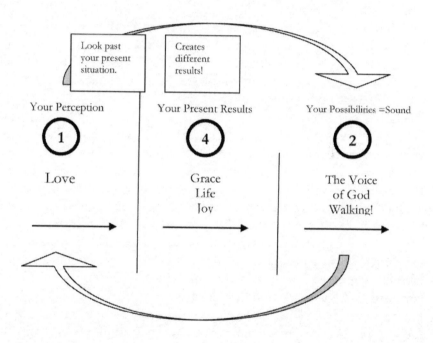

Thanksgiving is about ordering your perception. The effort here is to look past your present situation and create within your mind the results that you want despite what you see in front of you. So tithing has more to do with what's on your mind than actual finances. Within this, again, is the idea of returning to God, which means you take your cues from Heaven instead of Earth.

The Work of God's Spirit

In the Lord's Prayer it is stated, "thy will be done on earth as it is in heaven". To create on Earth, your cues have to be taken from heaven. So the information that comes from heaven is always and continuously available to you through the Spirit of God. As I said earlier, the Spirit of God hovered over the waters, and as it says in **Psalms 139**, the Spirit of God hovered over you in the womb. Notice that when you were in your mother's womb you were literally in water. One other point that I would like to bring out is that your physical structure contains 75% to 85% water. What does this mean?

To me, wherever water is, the Spirit of God is available to provide information for development. Don't take this lightly. Look at how a tree grows. Let's say an oak tree. As big and massive an oak tree can be, you would think that the ground in which the oak tree comes from would be displaced as the oak tree grows larger, thinking that the oak tree takes the substance from the ground around it. But this actually doesn't happen. The oak tree draws its substance from water. Somehow below the ground, instruction is given as to how the water should divide and take shape into a new existence by unfolding. All of this comes from the instructions as given by God through His Spirit.

So whatever circumstance you face, despite the conditions, there is always another story beyond what you see. The Spirit of God carries the true story and is present at all times to deliver to you the information needed for successful ends. This is what it means in **Psalms 139:16** that your members are written in the book of God and is developed continuously.

The word "book" denotes a narrative extended throughout the ages that counts your successful development at any given point in time. Again, you and I are fearfully and wonderfully made and our success has been established before the foundation of the world. So what is it that stops us at times from being successful?

It is simply what we think about – our tithes. If we go back to the word "hell", hell is how we approach life that extends into certain resulting conditions. It all comes from the mind. Remember, that the word hell in the Bible contains the connotation of hollowness in which I term "empty thinking". Hell is what we create. This is why David said, "Though I make my bed in hell, thou art there". Many times when we face situations or circumstances that are not in our best interest, we don't do a lot of thinking, mostly because we are unaware of the fact that we have the power to think and to arrange our thinking and thusly turning around our situations and circumstances. When we don't do this, when we don't hear God's Spirit, we are left in hell, then shortly thereafter our situations match our minds.

This is why the Bible says, "to enter into his Gates with Thanksgiving". Order your thoughts. Order your thinking. The Spirit is always available to create something new. Right-thinking creates right results. This is your financial bottom line. All money is structured after this pattern, because money is your mind and your mind is your money. Generally your financial circumstances reflect the state of your mind. This is why God in the book of Nehemiah used tithing as a model as to how to order your mind and to remind the people that they are His tithe. All of this comes by hearing God's Spirit.

Faith cometh by hearing, and Hearing by the Word or Sound of God.

The Sound of God

John 1:1-3

1 In the beginning was the Word, and the Word was with God, and the Word was God.

2 The same was in the beginning with God.

3 All things were made by him; and without him was not any thing made that was made.

Now let's look at a extended version of the chart we used earlier.

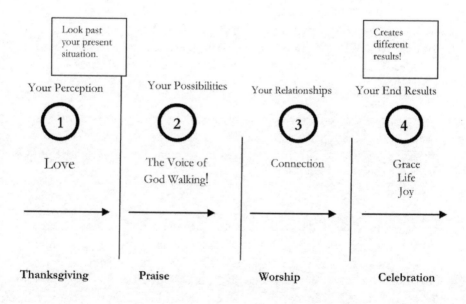

Praise is probably the most misunderstood concept in the modern history of Christianity. I want to employ a couple Scriptures here to help broaden the understanding of how praise truly works.

Zephaniah 3:17

The LORD thy God in the midst of thee [is] mighty; he will save, he will rejoice over thee with joy; he will rest in his love, he will joy over thee with singing.

Hebrew 2:11-12

For both he that sanctifieth and they who are sanctified [are] all of one: for which cause he is not ashamed to call them brethren, Saying, I will declare thy name unto my brethren, in the midst of the church will I sing praise unto thee.

A clue is set here in **Hebrews 2**, where Christ is speaking and saying, I will praise thee in the midst of the church or sanctuary. This leads one to the conclusion that after we enter into His Gates with Thanksgiving, Thanksgiving is then followed by Praise. But the praise here is not what you are doing towards God, but it is what Christ is doing towards you. This changes the whole equation of praise. Because praise starts with what Christ has to say about you and I, and then we respond accordingly.

This is where we generally miss the true understanding of the Word of God and the significance of how the Word of God works. According to **John 1:1**, "In the beginning was the Word and the Word was with God, and the Word was God. The same was in the beginning with God".

This clearly denotes that in the beginning there existed two Words. The Greek history of the word "Word" stems from the word "logos" meaning, to say or to speak. This leads me to believe that God's existence is a systemic presence of Sound, but not purposeless Sound, but a Sound that is in continuous conversation. This is a conversation that always lead to results. This is why it should be noted that the Word was in the beginning.

John 1:3

All things were made by him; and without him was not anything made that was made.

So by this conversation that existed in the beginning, all things were made. This makes sense as it is proclaimed in Isaiah:

Isaiah 55:11

So shall my word be that goeth forth out of my mouth: it shall not return unto me void, but it shall accomplish that which I please, and it shall prosper [in the thing] whereto I sent it.

But the conversation continues as we understand in **Colossians** chapter 3, that our lives are hid with Christ in God. **Ephesians 1** gives us a front row seat as to the breakdown of this conversation between the two Words of God.

Ephesians 1:5-6

⁵ Having predestinated us unto the adoption of children by Jesus Christ to himself, according to the good pleasure of his will,

⁶ To the praise of the glory of his grace, wherein he hath made us accepted in the beloved.

Here in **Ephesians 1:5** we see that it was decided by the Word beforehand that you and I was established by Christ in God according to the pleasure of His will and according to the praise of his glory as stated in the verse 6. Now before we move on any further and to really digest the full implication of God's praise towards us, we have to address the question of salvation.

Limiting Belief #9

We were born in sin and shaped in iniquity and therefore we stand in need of salvation and rescuing by God in order to make it to heaven. The same author of this statement also said that we are fearfully and wonderfully made, and that the thought of God towards you and I are precious. Which one is it? Which one would you like to believe?

Observation

Ephesians 1:6

To the praise of the glory of his grace, wherein he hath made us accepted in the beloved.

Here we clearly see that God has made us accepted in the beloved according to His Word. So if we add in what is stated in the book of Isaiah, "that His Word will not return void, but it shall accomplish what God pleases.", this leads me to understand quite clearly that our acceptance in Him is not predicated upon what we do, but it is predicated upon what God says - God's Sound. This also leads to the second of the four things that I said that you must know:

2. **Know the truth about where you are.**
   Meaning, know the true trajectory or place from which you oper ate from.

From reading the earlier verse of Ephesians chapter 1 we find this:

Ephesians 1:4

According as he hath chosen us in him before the foundation of the world, that we should be holy and without blame before him in love:

It clearly says that we were chosen in Him before the foundation of the world. If some people were condemned to hell, was this decided also before the foundation of the world? Nowhere is this found in the Bible. Based on **Ephesians 1:4** and **Ephesians 1:6**, we find that we were both chosen and accepted in God before the foundation of the world. Back to **Colossians 1:3**, "Our Life is hid with Christ in God". All of this was established by the Word, and we do know that the Word does not return void, and according to Hebrews, God does not change His mind.

So what actually happens here? Wherein is the issue of salvation? We read earlier that the fire tries every man's work, but he himself shall be saved. Here, I'm going to draw on what is probably the most famous Scripture as it concerns salvation.

Romans 10:9

That if thou shalt confess with thy mouth the Lord Jesus, and shalt believe in thine heart that God hath raised him from the dead, thou shalt be saved.

Let's take a closer look at the word "confess". The word "confess" is drawn from the Greek word "Homologeo". This word is a Greek compound word containing "Homo" and the word "logos". Homo means, together with or at the same time. "Logos" is defined as the Word or Sound of God. So drawn from the simple analogy of the word "confess" in which some say that it means to declare with the mouth, it is more correctly stated in this manner: our word is in agreement along with or together with the Word of God.

Here we find in the salvation Scripture a strong connotation of Praise along with the Word of God. Quite simply it means to be in agreement with the Word of God or simply say together along with the Word of God the same thing. But here you have to understand that Praise starts from God and not from you. So, life starts with hearing the Word of God and then speaking along with the Word of God.

Proverbs 18:21

Death and life [are] in the power of the tongue: and they that love it shall eat the fruit thereof.

Most religions have the habit of throwing the issue of life and death at the end of the world or when we die physically. But the issue of life and death is not determined "in the judgment" once you die. The issue of life and death is being determined within every moment of your life. The judgment is always current. The question of heaven and hell is not an end-of-life issue; it is a question of what's happening to you right now in your life. Can you master and command the things you want in life. Heaven is current. Hell is current. Salvation is not an issue of what happens after you die. The resurrection of Christ shows us the power that we have even after death. This power never goes away.

It is within what we think and thusly what we speak that determines our current condition of life and death, heaven and hell. Let's look at **John 3:7**, which is the next vital Scripture as it concerns the issue of salvation:

John 3:7

Marvel not that I said unto thee, Ye must be born again.

Born again here simply means to think from above or to regenerate from above. This means that you take your cues from heaven and not earth. "Thy will be done on earth as it is in heaven".

Philippians 3:20-21

20 For our conversation is in heaven; from whence also we look for the Saviour, the Lord Jesus Christ:

21 Who shall change our vile body, that it may be fashioned like unto his glorious body, according to the working whereby he is able even to subdue all things unto himself.

The key to salvation is a matter of changing the trajectory of your thinking. You either take your cues from Earth or the sounds of Earth, or you take cues from Heaven or the sounds from Heaven.

Colossians 3:1-2

If ye then be risen with Christ, seek those things which are above, where Christ sitteth on the right hand of God.

² Set your affection on things above, not on things on the earth.

Setting your affection has to do with your internal belief system. Here we deal with the second part of the Scripture of **Romans 10:9**... and shalt believe in thine heart that God hath raised him from the dead, thou shalt be saved.

Ephesians 2:4-6

⁴ But God, who is rich in mercy, for his great love wherewith he loved us,

⁵ Even when we were dead in sins, hath quickened us together with Christ, (by grace ye are saved;)

⁶ And hath raised us up together, and made us sit together in heavenly places in Christ Jesus:

I don't know if anybody pays particular attention to the fact that **Ephesians 2:6** uses the term "hath raised" and not "will raise". We diminish the work of Christ when we try to substitute the power of His words with our own distracted thinking. Somebody told us that there's a possibility that we can go to hell, and that's enough for people to believe it. This negates the Scriptures that clearly talk about on several occasions that we are "raised" and we are "seated", not "will sit", that we are seated together with Christ in heavenly places. "Together" in heavenly places. This is your true current state of residence.

Our True Residence

Now we have to face the importance of dealing with things on earth based on our true residence. It's not a matter of being saved or unsaved. It is a matter of knowing your true residence and believing that you can operate from the same standpoint that Christ operates.

It's like the story of the prodigal son. He had lost consciousness of his residence and then at his lowest point in hell he came back to his right mind. This is what it means to believe on Christ. It is setting your mind in the place where Christ exists and then aligning your Praise with His Praise. Aligning your praise with God's vocality or God's praise towards you moves you from the mental and physical state of hell. Return unto me and I will return unto you...

A lot of Christians have it hard today because they deal with life from a hollow space and place, believing that heaven is a place to get to and not a place where God has raised us up into therefore positioning us to operate from. So, even the very talk about hell and going to hell, or being banished to hell is a direct denial of the work of Christ and the Word of Christ. Quite literally, this denial leaves most Christians within the conditions of hell because of their lack of maturity to understand the Bible as it is clearly stated, that Christ will not lose one of us in **John 17**. It's as if there's an insatiable need to be punished. This is the height of sadomasochism, "beat me God, for I have sinned", "I don't deserve you Lord, for I am a wretched man in danger of hellfire, save me Lord!". We ask God to do what has already been done.

Your life is hid with Christ in God and that should be your point of operation. Now you must be born again, which simply means change the trajectory of your thinking from Earth to Heaven. Extending from Heaven is the Sound of God concerning your life, and how can the sound be anything other than "Good".

Come on people...think about it. Hell is what we cause ourselves now as an experience when we don't align ourselves with what is truly for us. Hell is not an everlasting punishment!

So what is grace?

Grace - The Sound That Outpaces Your Problems

This is my own personal definition of grace, but as you study God's Word and understand the power of believing in Christ as stated in **John 3**, you'll find that my definition of grace is highly accurate – it is the Sound of God that outpaces and stays ahead of your problems. So let's look at this chart again, starting with our perception or Thanksgiving.

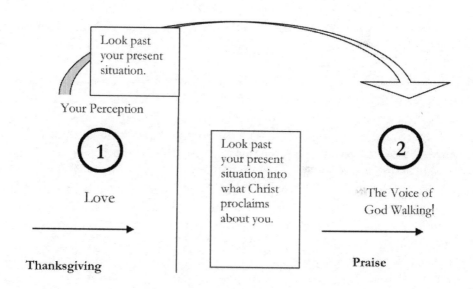

What Christ says about you despite your present circumstances or situation is Grace. Remember in **Psalms 139** that we are fearfully and wonderfully made and our members are written in His book. Remember also that the book denotes a narrative with the connotation of counting. What is counted here is the praise of Christ towards you beyond your situation, troubles, or what you're facing. Let me explain.

I was watching a documentary on TV that challenged the story of Moses and the children of Israel when they faced the Red Sea. At the time the Red Sea was in front of them with Pharaoh's army behind them. Left with nowhere to go, the children of Israel had to depend on an answer beyond themselves. God spoke to Moses and told him to stretch out the rod over the Red Sea. The Red Sea opened and the children of Israel crossed over safely on dry land.

The challenge of the show was to prove that the Red Sea experience was a natural occurrence within Earth's history. This would then disprove that a miracle took place at that point. What was found was that every so many millions of years the Earth would slightly tilt on its axis. The documentary pinpointed and proved the time of the tilt coincides with the time that the children of Israel had to cross the Red Sea. This would explain the Red Sea moving back. But what would determine the dry ground or explain the dry ground?

Studies also show that every 27,000 years or so there would be an east wind that would blow in that region systematically. So it was said that these two events just so happened to take place at the same time. In order for these two separate events to cross paths with their own historical timelines, it would take billions of years where the dating and time would coincide. Now the numbers that I am giving here, I estimated based on the best of my memory. But what was proven here was that over an expansive time the Red Sea experience was a natural occurrence within Earth's history that was set to happen anyway without God's intervention.

I guess the television producer's aim was to prove that the forces behind this occurrence were not conjured up at that moment when Moses stretched his rod over the sea. Frankly, I agree with them. And by agreeing with them, I trust in the billion year scenario. But this to me proves an even bigger miracle. This would mean that billions of years before the event happened, God had planned for their deliverance.

It would suffice to say that way back in Earth's history, God through his personal narrative had already counted out the days within milliseconds in order to time out what was the "good" that was to happen at that very moment. Here science proved that God's mind and God's thought was situated billions of years before Moses faced his dilemma. Now imagine when you face a perceived issue or problem the amount of things that are set right by God billions of years before you reach that moment in time.

This is the Sound of God meeting you at every moment. This is what it means, that where sin abounds, Grace much more abounds.

When you are facing personal struggles and trials, the idea is not to focus on that, but to focus on the Vocality of God that existed before the foundation of the world that concerned you before you met your trouble. This is the narrative counting of God, the documenting of your success before your failures even appear in your presence. This is the grace of God. This is the sound of God. Just beyond your problem is a Praise towards you. Let's look at it this way: at His name, every knee shall bow and every tongue shall confess…this includes the knee of hell!

What's God's Name

Psalms 138:2

I will worship toward thy holy temple, and praise thy name for thy lovingkindness and for thy truth: for thou hast magnified thy word above all thy name.

It is said here that the Word of God is magnified above the name of God. What is the name of God?

Exodus 3:13-14

[13] *And Moses said unto God, Behold, when I come unto the children of Israel, and shall say unto them, The God of your fathers hath sent me unto you; and they shall say to me, What is his name? what shall I say unto them?*

[14] *And God said unto Moses, I AM THAT I AM: and he said, Thus shalt thou say unto the children of Israel, I AM hath sent me unto you.*

So we see here that God's name is I AM THAT I AM. Let me show you the formula.

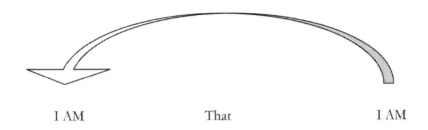

I AM   That   I AM

God is always on the other side of what you're facing. Life, again, is about unfolding. You might have a situation that has unfolded in front of you that you did not like or was not to your satisfaction, but you can rest assure that beyond that present moment, God is declaring his Name into the Earth as His Word is above His name. So beyond your problem God counted into your being an answer that was called into existence before the foundation of the world by God's own vocal narrative. That's why it states in **Ephesians 1** that we are blessed with all spiritual blessings, not just some spiritual blessings.

The book has been written. You and I have been counted victorious over our chaos at every turn. This is a done deal. His name is just beyond your problem and His name rests in your recognition (thinking from above) that His name is who you are and how you chose to respond. If you are His image, you are His name and the end result of His name is always good based on his Word.

The issue is never God's work in you, but you recognizing and then believing in the work of God.

1 Corinthians 15:58

*Therefore, my beloved brethren, be ye stedfast, unmoveable, **always abounding in the work** of the Lord, forasmuch as ye know that your labour is not in vain in the Lord.*

Non-recognition of the work leaves you in hell, or in a hollow, fiery place. When God said "I AM" that...He is speaking "I AM" into the earth. Now you have to choose to live "I Am" beyond what is not. This is where we check back into the concept of sorrow. Sorrow as in without form and void, chaos, or what you face at times which is disturbing, what makes you uncomfortable, what's growing old, what's decaying, and what's not working... It simply means it's time to move on to a new level.

Sorrow is not a concept created to hurt you, sorrow is just a sensation that when responded to right, it will take you to the next level. In order for God to grow into more, God Himself had to say less is not enough. So know your place, and your place is not in hell, but your place is in Heaven.

1 Corinthians 15:49

And as we have borne the image of the earthy, we shall also bear the image of the heavenly.

You and I are the only created life existence that is both earthly and heavenly. Earth reflects Heaven. This is the purpose of life. Life does not start with your existence here on Earth, it starts with your existence in Heaven, and as Christ praises you, you should answer that praise with like praise. Just as everything produces after its kind in nature, you are to produce after God's kind into the Earth. God's Word is complete in Heaven, but is yet to be developed fully on Earth. You become more of the image of God as you hear His praise, and then you regenerate His praise for production.

2 Corinthians 3:18

But we all, with open face beholding as in a glass the glory of the Lord, are changed into the same image from glory to glory, [even] as by the Spirit of the Lord.

Now you can fully begin to understand the work of the Spirit as it hovers over every one of your circumstances. The work of the Spirit is to provide information that moves you and I to new heights in every moment. Those new heights are always predesigned and counted out by God on your behalf, waiting for you to hear your name "I AM" that exist beyond what you need to get past or get over. This is just the simple extension of the creation and development process that formed the foundation of the world that we all live in.

Ephesians 1:11-12

11 In whom also we have obtained an inheritance, being predestinated according to the purpose of him who worketh all things after the counsel of his own will:

12 That we should be to the praise of his glory, who first trusted in Christ.

Who trusted in Christ? God trusted in Christ. God trusted in the Word of Christ concerning you. Now you have to trust in the same Voice.

Ephesians 1:13-14

13 In whom ye also trusted, after that ye heard the word of truth, the gospel of your salvation: in whom also after that ye believed, ye were sealed with that holy Spirit of promise,

14 Which is the earnest of our inheritance until the redemption of the purchased possession, unto the praise of his glory.

You were sealed with the Holy Spirit of promise. Therefore the inheritance belongs to you. Now wake up and go back home... Return to God... This is your true place and your true residence.

The vibration is sealed.

The song of success is sung.

The energy is set into completeness.

Move past not enough into living His Name, which is the higher sounding you.

The Anatomy of Worship

Worship is not something you do in church; worship extends from you as a state of being. This state of being lays the groundwork for great things to happen to you and around you. I see it as this:

Wor-ship
the
Word Shipped

Worship is when you're capable of getting the Word of God out through your state of being. Worship is connection with God that becomes readily visible to others, having a deep impact on how others experience God through you. It is delivering the Word of God as people witness your possibilities turn into reality. I would dare say, Worship is the mastery and command of what you want in life. This is the Word returning that's not void.

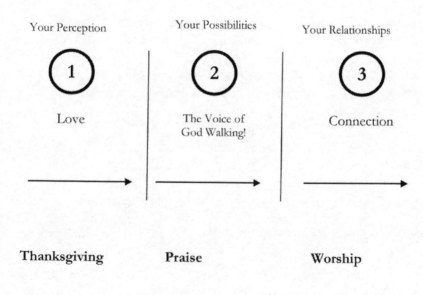

Your Perception	Your Possibilities	Your Relationships
1	**2**	**3**
Love	The Voice of God Walking!	Connection

Thanksgiving   **Praise**   **Worship**

Worship is built on the quality of the relationships that you have that creates an energy around you that is positive and constructive. After Thanksgiving, and then after Praise, you enter into Worship. This is where you find a superior connection with God and others, but not a meaningless connection, or a "spiritual" connection. This is a type of connection that produces results, and your results incites a response from others as they witness Heaven being produced through you here on Earth. This is Worship. Worship is your connection that lead to production.

John 4:23-24

23 But the hour cometh, and now is, when the true worshippers shall worship the Father in spirit and in truth: for the Father seeketh such to worship him.

24 God is a Spirit: and they that worship him must worship him in spirit and in truth.

The Spirit is what God says. The Truth is what's produced based on what God said. In order for God to produce what He said, He was in a right relationship. Using this as a map for your purpose, you can restate this as follows:

The Spirit is what you think and thusly say based on what you want. The Truth is what you produce based on what you say. In order to produce what you want, you must be in right relationships. This brings us to our third truth:

3. Know the truth about your relationships.
Know the state of your relationships and connections.

Nothing functions without relationships. The entire ecosystem is just that, an ecosystem of relationships which serve as the basis of all functionality. When you take a detailed look at Earth's development in Genesis 1, you will find that embedded into all of creation is a series of relationships, and growth only takes place when relationships are optimized.

You cannot take for granted your current relationships. Your relationships are the basis for your rise or your fall, your ability to produce or not to produce. In Biblical tradition, if a woman who was sexually consummating her marriage, had a man whose performance sexually was weak, she was to immediately leave that man and go through the town crying out that the man was unworthy, and to warn other women about his weakness. You see, if a man performed poorly sexually, it also meant he was weak economically and he would produce poor seed. Even the children would turn out weak.

The woman was then to leave that man and find another man who was a strong producer. This was the basis of the story of the women at the well. She had five husbands and the one she currently had, he was not for her. Most people read this story as if the woman was promiscuous. This is far from the truth. She was doing what was custom! When the relationship had the potential of being sorry, she had to leave!

There should be no room in your life for weak relationships. If the core of your life's purpose is to produce, then you cannot afford any type of relationship that does not lead to optimal production. You must have a strong practice of leaving what doesn't work. This is why many people feel an emptiness at the core of their being. They are "in love" with someone, or attached to someone, but that someone is weak in their constitution towards production. People stay in these unfruitful relationships trying to "work it out". I got news for you! It will never happen.

If you are in a relationship; it could be a husband, wife, boyfriend, girlfriend, best friend, coworker, a job, and even family, if it is not producing anything, GET OUT! The core of your "Godness" is production and all production starts with relationship. If you are busy fixing your relationship, you are wasting your mind and time. True relationships are about building. Time spent fixing is time taken away from building. Let me save you some money with the psychologist, psychiatrist, and marriage counselor: Leave!

You have to treasure the value of production and the fulfillment that it leads to. Many people are looking to be fulfilled and try to do it by fixing the person they are with. It's simple; everybody must bring their best to the table. If not, dinner can't be served. If either you or the person you're with is not willing to do this, there is no true love. It makes no sense to pretend that there is love, and go off just the feeling that you are in love. Your relationship becomes a lie!

A young lady who had a boyfriend was telling me how much she was "in love" with him. I explained to her that she wasn't. She shot back at me, "Yes I am, you can't tell me how I feel"! I said to her, "No I can't, but I can tell what's real". Your feelings are based off of what he has said". She said, "How do you know?" As I stood in her apartment, I told her I don't see him. To be in love you have to live in his love and I don't see him.

Nothing in her apartment reflected that she had a man in her life. I saw no impact that he was having on her. It takes a weak man to say that he loves someone and there's no physicality that follows it. When you are in a relationship, the purpose of your relationship should extend from your own personal purpose. Reaching out and investing anything into anybody who is not investing into you in an optimal way is the practice of poverty. You cannot be in love without actually being "in" love.

Most corporations follow this same philosophy. If you are not providing what leads to more growth, you are fired! Why should we manage any of our personal relationships in any other way?

No. This is not a hard line. There is always room for improvement, but when an individual within the context of any type of relationship refuses to grow or contribute based on his or her ability, it will cause everybody in the whole equation to lose. The whole system churns in cycles of death and non-production. Life is about building and growing. Let's take a closer look.

Body Building

There are four words that can be used interchangeably in the Bible. They are as follows:

Body - Temple - City - Kingdom

All these are representations of who you are in the earth. It is these entities that God looks to build on Earth as a representation of what's in Heaven. As it concerns the Temple representing who you are, the following scripture becomes very important and central to your spiritual makeup and your ability to live a successful life here on Earth by God's Spirit.

1 Corinthians 6:19-20

¹⁹ What? know ye not that your body is the temple of the Holy Ghost which is in you, which ye have of God, and ye are not your own?

²⁰ For ye are bought with a price: therefore glorify God in your body, and in your spirit, which are God's.

2 Corinthians 3:17-18

¹⁷ Now the Lord is that Spirit: and where the Spirit of the Lord is, there is liberty.

¹⁸ But we all, with open face beholding as in a glass the glory of the Lord, are changed into the same image from glory to glory, even as by the Spirit of the Lord.

This is how we glorify God in our body, by beholding our own image who is Christ and growing from glory to glory. Now to understand the nature of the body or bodies that we have control over which unfolds over time, we have to go back to the concept of what we should understand in the first book of Genesis as the process of creating "after its kind". Whatever seed is planted in the ground unfolds into more of what it is. This is a body. Look at this question that is asked in **1st Corinthians 15:35**.

1 Corinthians 15:35

But some [man] will say, How are the dead raised up? and with what body do they come?

Remember, without retaining the knowledge of God, we operate from a point of hollowness which is hell. God desires that we are raised up from this condition so we can produce after His kind. So a seed must die to become more.

1 Corinthians 15:36-38

36 Thou fool, that which thou sowest is not quickened, except it die:

37 And that which thou sowest, thou sowest not that body that shall be, but bare grain, it may chance of wheat, or of some other grain:

38 But God giveth it a body as it hath pleased him, and to every seed his own body.

1 Corinthians 15:43-44

43 It is sown in dishonour; it is raised in glory: it is sown in weakness; it is raised in power:

44 It is sown a natural body; it is raised a spiritual body. There is a natural body, and there is a spiritual body

So a body is created based on the seed that is planted.

Note: When churches and ministries tell people to plant a financial seed into their ministry and that this "planting" will result into a future blessing from God; this is a gross misrepresentation of God's teaching on seed time and harvest. Jesus represents the seed, and you and I are the harvest and continued seed. To take this teaching and try to retrofit it into a teaching about giving money to a church or a ministry is an outright misrepresentation that parlays into a line of poverty and continued suffering, in which people then continue to give more money with the hope of getting out of their situations.

The body that is grown or growing from the seed is you and I, and this is a result of God planting His seed into the Earth so that you and I can grow based on the DNA structures of who He is and what's contained in Him. This is bodybuilding. Christ is the first fruit, and from the first fruit comes the rest of the fruit. How dare a ministry make this a matter of money with the promise of God blessing you at a later date if you give them money, which in general, never really happens for a lot of people.

Just as a tree reflects what's in the seed, we reflect what's in Christ. So bodybuilding is about reflecting your source. Not only is this how growth should take place in our own lives, but we see this model embedded into all of creation as everything produces after its kind.

Temple Building and City Building

The temple and the city as found in the Bible are bodies that also represent your personal existence. When it comes to the Temple, I can go into great detail as to what the different facets within the Temple represent and how each can serve as a model to improve your life and your relationships. But what I want to focus on here is the subject of relationship, and so I want to concentrate on what both the Temple and the city has in common. They both have 12 gates, three gates on each of the four sides of its structure.

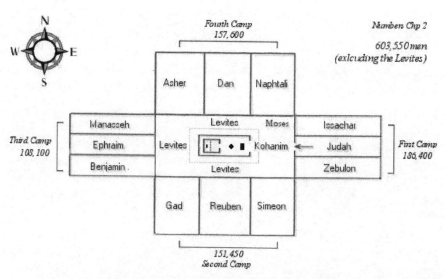

These gates for me take on a special meaning, especially as it concerns the command to enter His Gates with Thanksgiving. If the Temple or the city represents your personal body, or better stated your personal energy system, then you must protect what comes into your gates. At every moment you're connecting with someone, but your connections should always lead to profitable results and growth.

A lot of times when you are left feeling empty, it is based on the quality and quantity of the relationships that you build and accept in your life. So we understand that our bodies are the temple of the Holy Ghost and what takes place in the Temple preserves the body. So what enters into your Temple or your space that is vital? This means you must take measurement of every relationship that you form. Because with every relationship you either add to your life or diminish your life. Let's look at the following Scripture.

1 Corinthians 15:33

Be not deceived: evil communications corrupt good manners.

This simply means evil company corrupts good results. When you're not achieving good results in your life, many times it can be attributed to the direct relationships that you have. It takes great relationships to accomplish anything, but a lot of times at the core of your being, you feel that you have something missing. What you have to do here is to take stock in the exchanges that you make on a daily basis. Every exchange you make should lead to growth. This is the only basis for true Worship.

I realized that connected into everyone's personal energy system are 12 gates that lead to the core of your well-being. So I have designed a system to help you to recognize what I call the *12 Points of Significance* that you should use as a measuring tool to maintain a healthy energy body through your relationships. People must enter into your gates with Thanksgiving, and you must protect your gates if they're not willing to provide the proper investment towards you for your personal growth. This is building your Temple or your City.

Your true economy starts with your relationship with others and their relationship towards you. It feels good when people can respond to your needs and your purpose. It is even better when people see your needs and respond to you without you even having to ask. It is even greater when people are so tuned into you that they meet your need before it even becomes a need. This not only gives you significance, but because energy is not spent here "fixing", you are immediately enabled to see "the more" in your life and move to your next levels due to people having your best interest at heart. Every time a need is put to rest, when something is accomplished through partnership, when people agree with you and move in the same direction along with you, and when things are completed, that existence becomes minted or coined into reality. So a person's Thanksgiving towards you is vital.

Your economy starts with your relationship with others.

Whenever you have been rested one level, the next level is already there waiting for your systemic aggregation of relationships to bring what you're looking for into reality or into the reality of your desired experience - which is a good experience. True intimacy is not about having to think about "how to", because your relationship "machine" is so responsive to you, that the difference between thinking and manifesting becomes seamless. This is a sure way to master and command what you want in life. People must line up with what God has called in your life.

Your five senses should be used as a source of confirmation of these processes and not to gain information for mere survival. When you don't reach for what's inside you to determine your significance, then you reach for things and people outside yourself to do this job in order make you feel significant. Your significance then is left at the mercy of other people's behavior verses it being designed by you and then having other people coming into agreement with your personal design. People entering into your gates that is not lined up to your values will defile your temple.

This is crucial to the point of salvation that we talked about earlier. As you agree with the Praise extended towards you by God, everyone in your life must come into agreement with the same Word.

2 Corinthians 6:14

Be ye not unequally yoked together with unbelievers: for what fellowship hath righteousness with unrighteousness? and what communion hath light with darkness?

True significance starts on the inside, then matched on the outside.

They are as follows:

The 12 Points of Significance

1
(To Be Viewed)
The Investment of seeing and knowing a person.

- To know a person as in their habits, favorite things, concerns etc.
- To be concerned and having a person's back based on what you see in them.
- See, recognize, and care for one's issues.

Everyone needs someone to see and know who they are.

2
(To Be Comprehended)
The Investment of understanding a person.

- Understanding of one's issues.
- Willing to take in right information concerning a person.
- Agreement and right action towards that understanding of the person.

Everyone has a need to be understood.

3
(To Be Engaged)
The Investment of active commitment.

- Physical connection.
- Partnership and unification.
- Two way exchange or communication.

Everyone has a need to be touched in some way.

4
(To Be Praised)
The Investment of vocal affirmation of the good.

- Recognition and hearing about good attributes.
- Complimentary in nature towards a person.
- Approvals of ideas, thoughts, visions...etc.

Everyone has a need to hear something good about themselves.

5
(To Be Believed)
The Investment of trust.

- Take a position based on concerns verbalized, or character exuded.
- Action oriented belief qualified by action oriented support.
- Taking responsibility and acting on a person's behalf based believing in them.

Everyone has a need to be trusted and believed in.
6

(To Be Prioritized)
The Investment of making one special.

- Acute attention in certain situations and areas.
- Putting things aside in recognition of the other.
- Allowing a person from time to time to be the most important.

Everyone has the need to feel number one sometimes.

7

(To Be Enriched)
The Investment of provision.

- Bringing gifts or supplies not associated with earning.
- Sharing your personal substance.
- Making sure a person's needs are met.

Everyone has a need to receive.

8

(To Be Advanced)
The Investment of pushing one forward.

- Progressing one's effort by means of time and efforts.
- Providing leadership in your area of expertise to advance the cause of another.
- To give an effort in setting a situation or circumstance right.

Everyone has a need to be mentored or pushed forward.

9

(To Be Rewarded)
The Investment of recognition.

- To provide substance in recognition of what someone has invested in you.
- Physical substance given in appreciation for efforts made.
- Thank you and appreciation outside of verbal affirmation.

Everyone has a need to be appreciated in a tangible way.

10
(To Be Exalted)
The Investment of one's self into another.

- Time spent in all areas of emotional investments.
- Giving a sense of place based on your presence.
- The gift of yourself that lift a person to another level, give status or empowers.

Everyone has a need to feel another's presence that builds their own presence.

11
(To Be Increased)
The Investment of addition.

- To empower, enhance or enable in any way.
- To see then add in a positive way time, effort, or substance.
- To be an extension for someone where someone comes short.

Everyone has a need to be completed by the investment of another's effort and partnership.

12
(To Be Doubled)
The Investment of multiplication.

- The experience of results.
- Results that lead to more results.
- Results that give a sense of place, home, completeness.

Everyone has a need to grow by the investment of another's effort or partnership.

As you can see, your relationships and how they are set, play a vital role in your ability to see and experience your life at its best. This is the true beginning of everything economic. In order to live a fuller and more exiting life you must prepare yourself to receive your full supply of what's for you by setting your perception and aligning your relationships in order to keep focused on your own good and producing good.

Kingdom Building

I want to make sure that you really get the point of this book. We all have the power in this life to get what we want. Nothing is left up to unseen forces that are working without your knowledge impacting your life without your control. Let me make that clear. You have full mastery and command over your own life. This is a design set by God as you image who He is.

Limiting Belief #10

A good number of people believe that there are forces, mainly Satan and his angelic host, that are constantly battling you in the unseen. Thusly, when anything goes wrong in life, it can quickly be attributed to these forces that God is "allowing" for the time being to take place in this divine drama called life. They also believe, with this being the case that

God and Christ are set up as a rescue mission and team to come in as needed to deliver people from "the enemy". Then once we "overcome" one thing, the process starts all over again. This can't be further from the truth.

Observation

This whole notion is far from the truth. As matter fact, this warps our whole perception as to how life really works and weakens our ability to produce what we really want in life. On both ends; first, the belief in the battling evil forces, and secondly, the belief that God rescues us as He sees fit, it becomes easy to pass on responsibility as to what happens in your life to this misinterpreted unseen world of good and evil forces.

Here is one scripture that seems to lead us in that direction:

Ephesians 6:12

For we wrestle not against flesh and blood, but against principalities, against powers, against the rulers of the darkness of this world, against spiritual wickedness in high [places].

This makes it seems as though life is one big struggle against the devil and therefore you need a savior and to be saved from these unseen monsters. Can you imagine? God creates the world just so this divine drama can play out over thousands of years, with many humans losing the battle and succumbing to the will of this most powerful angel named Lucifer. Lucifer gets the advantage by influencing only one woman and one man to eat a piece of fruit. Now the rest of us are "born in sin and shaped in iniquity", which then puts us at a great disadvantage, and in the fight for our life for all of our life.

It is thought that because of this we are now subject to things not working. We are subject to things failing. We are subject to things going wrong. We are subject to wanting things and not getting it, and we are subject to having a part of our lives exposed to the will of the evil one. So all of this just becomes "the way it is", and our hope is found in a

God "sitting high and looking down low", waiting for you and I to submit to Him before we can be rescued from the works of the devil. Even then, we are told, it gets harder because we have "given our life to the Lord" and "the enemy" is now mad. Because of our faith, the devil is now turning up the volume on his devices, and is putting in that extra push to get us to fail in our Christian walk.

What a life!!!! Get this. This drama doesn't end for mankind until Jesus comes again. While we wait, a good number of people die in their sins and go to hell. What's funny about this whole divine drama, it cost you 10% of your income just to go to church to find out how you can win!!!

Wait! If you don't pay, you don't have to worry about the devil. God will curse you Himself!

This is the Christian drama. Some will win, and some will lose. Is all of this true?

First, let's look at this word "wrestle" in **Ephesians 6:12**. The Greek translation that shows up here is the word "vibrate" and not the word wrestle. This changes the whole psychological trajectory of the matter and sets in a new and more correct perception and perspective.

The energy of evil forces is not designed to come against you as an opponent, but these forces vibrates in tandem with you as you make your decisions, mainly decisions that are negative. So you see a set of unseen forces, principalities, powers, and rulers of darkness that is set to vibrate after your order. BUT KNOW THIS!

You set the order (period!).

You make the decisions. You hear your Praise and you either agree with it, or disagree with it.

You set your relationships.

Your results then unfold. (period!).

The Misunderstood Kingdom

Most people will never ask, what is the Kingdom? What is the Kingdom of Heaven? Today's religious standards proclaim that the kingdom of Heaven is just that, a kingdom. People align the Biblical kingdom with movies about the old kingdoms of England, the ancient empires of China and old Egyptian dynasties. They then try to interpret the Bible from this modern point of understanding.

As it then concerns building God's kingdom versus the kingdoms that are played out in the movies, a spiritual application is drawn from this viewpoint of what a kingdom is. With this, it is considered that the Biblical kingdom has a ruler, its court, and then its subjects. Here, God Himself is the supreme ruler and we are the subjects. A kingdom according to our current understanding also involves having territories and provinces. So when there is talk about building the kingdom of God, it is generally understood that it involves this type of structure.

Along with being God's subjects, there is a concern with the building local ministries or churches as they are local representations of the territories and provinces of God. Building the kingdom of God is also seen as adding more subjects through "soul winning" and expanding local ministries through your financial support. As these functionalities must be maintained or expanded, it is considered to be valor to work for "the kingdom". Don't do the work in the King's kingdom, you're thrown into the King's dungeon (hell).

The Kingdom – A Practice not a Place

The true kingdom of Heaven is a practice and not a place. A kingdom as translated in the New Testament of the Bible is actually not a kingdom as we know it at all. The word that shows up in the Greek is "Basileia" which means royal power or "crowned" power. The kingdom of Heaven has everything to do with the power that comes from your mind. As you continue to trace the history of the word "kingdom" in the Bible, you will also find "leader of people" or commander. Commander of what? Commander of your ability to produce based on the foundation that you create or choose. The same goes for a city or any building, it has to have a foundation. The base of the word "Basileia" is both Greek and English, which is "Basis", which means to step or walking, that which one steps, and the foot.

Kingdom! Stop! Get this. This is the word that is the original translation of "Kingdom" - Baseleia. If you miss this, the whole trajectory of your thinking will lead you in a direction that is fruitless, and every point in the New Testament where the word "kingdom" shows up, if understood wrong, will throw you into a severe misdirection of your ability to image God on Earth, because the kingdom of Heaven is about your ability to produce "God" into the physical. To produce after His kind.

This power of the Kingdom is set for you to master and command your desires into existence. We cannot play patty-cake with this, we are no longer in the romper room of Christianity and must mature into what works and not carry these elementary ideas of God's purpose for our lives.

Yes, this is a major change in the known Spiritual structure for most people, but we cannot deal with the Kingdom from a misunderstood standpoint.

Kingdom- The Seat of Your Personal Power

I took a poll and I will boldly stand in any church and take a poll. We have to. I asked at a Bible study at a church in Florida. "How many people have a special need from God wherein they were praying for this need over the past six months?" Every hand went up, and I mean every hand. Six months? Wow.

The next question. How many of you are faithful in paying your tithes? About 50%-60% of their hands went up. Now speaking to those tithe payers, I asked, "How many of you received an answer to your prayers within the last six months?" NO HANDS WENT UP! I told the people, this is not the power of God and it is time to get on to some real truth about how God works.

Telling them that they reflect who God is in the Earth was foreign to them. Telling them that they had the mind of Christ was foreign to them. Telling them that they were chosen in God before the foundation of the world to the Praise of his Glory was foreign to them. Telling them that they were fearfully and wonderfully made was a distant idea to them. Telling them that God was going to never lose them was almost blasphemous, because they believed in hell. My heart broke as they believed and served a God that was weaker than their circumstances.

They believed that you have to "chase" after God. God said, "I will never leave you nor forsake you". They believed that you had to praise God to maintain His attention, not realizing that He praises us, calling out the good in our lives. They believed that if God had a Kingdom, that He was a King and that they were naturally lower than He was which naturally throws out the whole notion of being made in His image. They believed that the devil and his angels were in a constant war with them, so the Christian life was to be a struggle without recognizing that Christ said, "My yoke is easy and my burdens are light, and as far as invisible angelic powers, He has put all things under our feet."

Psalms 91:13

Thou shalt tread upon the lion and adder: the young lion and the dragon shalt thou trample under feet.

Psalms 8:4-6

⁴ What is man, that thou art mindful of him? and the son of man, that thou visitest him?

⁵ For thou hast made him a little lower than the angels, and hast crowned him with glory and honour.

⁶ Thou madest him to have dominion over the works of thy hands; thou hast put all things under his feet:

Romans 16:20

And the God of peace shall bruise Satan under your feet shortly. The grace of our Lord Jesus Christ [be] with you. Amen.

Hebrews 2:6-9

6 But one in a certain place testified, saying, What is man, that thou art mindful of him? or the son of man that thou visitest him?

7 Thou madest him a little lower than the angels; thou crownedst him with glory and honour, and didst set him over the works of thy hands:

8 Thou hast put all things in subjection under his feet. For in that he put all in subjection under him, he left nothing that is not put under him. But now we see not yet all things put under him.

9 But we see Jesus, who was made a little lower than the angels for the suffering of death, crowned with glory and honour; that he by the grace of God should taste death for every man.

Watch this:

Ephesians 1:18-23

18 The eyes of your understanding being enlightened; that ye may know what is the hope of his calling, and what the riches of the glory of his inheritance in the saints,

19 And what is the exceeding greatness of his power to us-ward who believe, according to the working of his mighty power,

20 Which he wrought in Christ, when he raised him from the dead, and set him at his own right hand in the heavenly places,

21 Far above all principality, and power, and might, and dominion, and every name that is named, not only in this world, but also in that which is to come:

²² And hath put all things under his feet, and gave him to be the head over all things to the church,

²³ Which is his body, the fulness of him that filleth all in all.

So this is the story of Man and Christ. But just in case you think Christ is the only one in Heaven with this privilege, watch this:

Ephesians 2:5-7

⁵ Even when we were dead in sins, hath quickened us together with Christ, (by grace ye are saved;)

⁶ And hath raised us up together, and made us sit together in heavenly places in Christ Jesus:

⁷ That in the ages to come he might shew the exceeding riches of his grace in his kindness toward us through Christ Jesus.

Colossians 3:3

For ye are dead, and your life is hid with Christ in God.

This is why it's important to know your place so you can use the right mind to obtain the things you want in life.

Colossians 3:1-2

If ye then be risen with Christ, seek those things which are above, where Christ sitteth on the right hand of God.

² Set your affection on things above, not on things on the earth.

So, all things are placed under our feet by default. So where you and I "walk", where our feet are, is above all the angelic host. This leads us right back to the meaning of "Kingdom". You control both what is seen and what is unseen. That's why there is no battle between forces in the unseen. Christ is the Author and Finisher of our Faith, so now you must be about the business of authoring your own life. With this corrected understanding of what the kingdom is, I'm going to use the "Kingdom" principals to establish 12 foundations for your success. These are the 12 foundations you need in order to master and command what you want in life.

The 12 Foundations of Success

Seek ye first the Kingdom
(Matthew 6:33)...

Keep yourself within focus.

Never down play your own value. Most people are distracted and distance from developing themselves. They try to get what they want in life without "getting" themselves. Without self-knowledge it becomes difficult to gain in life or to add to your life. The Kingdom of Heaven is you.

Deliver the Kingdom to its Source
(1st Corinthians 15:20-28)...

Keep your focus on your end results.

1 Corinthians 15:24

Then [cometh] the end, when he shall have delivered up the kingdom to God, even the Father; when he shall have put down all rule and all authority and power.

This actually brings your fourth truth:

4. Know the truth about your results.
Take measurement of your results. All results are a physical picture of your spiritual world.

The end comes when you tithe, meaning to return to God. You wake up. When you come back home (heaven - your rightful place) or deliver the kingdom to God which is you, you bring whatever matter in front of you to an end - **1st Corinthians 15:24**. This means to think from a higher point of consciousness which is above what you are facing, trying to complete, or overcome. How do you put what's in front of you under you? You have a mind to determine a different end - think from above. When you try to fix what's in front of you, you will come to an end versus what's in front of you coming to an end.

The strategy is to move your mind to a higher place, which then places what's in front of you under your feet. You are the leader of your circumstances. Do not let your circumstances lead you. When your mind reaches the point of determining what you want over and above what you don't want (sorrow) that brings the matter to an end. The seed then dies and will be raised into what you want. Unfolding (substance).

You see these types of people all the time. Their mind is in a different place. They are undaunted by what's in front of them, because to them, they have already accomplished what they are going for. They have already reached an end and feel within the depths of their souls with great expectation that things will unfold exactly how they planned it. Everything produces after its kind.

This is where life puts death to death.

1 Corinthians 15:25-26

25 For he must reign, till he hath put all enemies under his feet.

26 The last enemy that shall be destroyed is death.

To stay focused, anything around that is dead must be destroyed. God responds to your focus and not your distractions. Distractions are deadly against anything you try to do. Herein the true power to the Kingdom:

1 Corinthians 15:27-28

27 For he hath put all things under his feet. But when he saith all things are put under him, it is manifest that he is excepted, which did put all things under him.

28 And when all things shall be subdued unto him, then shall the Son also himself be subject unto him that put all things under him, that God may be all in all.

Yes. That's exactly what it says. When you subdue these things, the Son Himself becomes subject to you, that God may be all in all. For God to be God, you must be successful, and that's why He gave His Son, so we can have life and life more abundantly.

The Kingdom is like a Pearls
(Matthew 13:44-46)...

Give what you want all you got.

When you face sorrow and sorrow gets the best of you, it simply means that what you want in life, you do not want it bad enough. Some say it's a matter of believing in what you can do. I say it's a matter of what you think that you might have to give up in order to get what you want. You are afraid to lose some things in order to gain something.

What you have to lose becomes central to your thinking. That's why I don't believe in teaching hell, because it propagates the possibility of losing, and you can carry this mindset into your recognition of your own potential because preservation becomes your point of focus instead of living the life you are blessed with. Think about it, most of Christian philosophy is based on preservation because you have to try "win" or gain salvation or you will lose.

If you start with salvation as being a fact, no circumstantial situation in front of you becomes a matter of determination. People win when they are sure about what they have, so what they need to get rid of in order to experience of what they want doesn't become a matter of consideration. They just go for it.

Tyler Perry knew the pearl and treasure that he had and was willing to sleep in his car so his every resource was tuned into his dream. Now he is worth millions and is living the life he wants. Mostly every successful person doesn't mind being broke while they go for broke.

Stop pussyfooting around and do what's needed to get what you want.

The Kingdom is like Wheat with Weeds
(Matthew 13:24-39, 47-50)...

Keep acting on your focus.

The tares or weeds in this story represents a distraction, so the instruction was, was to not pull them up. Do not spend time on the tares or the weeds. Do not spend time answering the things that are wrong. Distraction is a severely underestimated life existence and practice, because most times you are distracted without notice. Turning away from your intent redirects your intent, thusly redirecting your results.

When you have determined a direction or a desire, your mind will be immediately introduced to many other possibilities. This is the nature of sorrow. When "I can" comes to mind, the "what ifs" show up also. Any goal that you set in your mind is like an airport terminal, many other thoughts like weeds will fly in with it. This is natural. Even though that distracting thought exist, you do not have to answer it or jump on its flight. Stay on the plane headed towards what you want.

Any distraction distances you from acting on what you want. Distraction equals Dis-action. Let them be. As in both of these parables, when you reach a determination, what you don't need will actually be burned off in the end. Do not stop what you are doing to take time to pull up the weeds.

The Kingdom is like Ten Virgins
(Matthew 25:1-13)...

Keep moving towards your focus. Stay on Purpose.

Never go backwards to answer something that doesn't matter, or you will miss what does matter. Most believe that the problem the five foolish virgins had was that they were unprepared because they had no oil in their lamps. Yes, this was a fact but it wasn't a problem. Their purpose was to meet the bridegroom.

When the call went out to meet the bridegroom, the foolish five went to go get oil for their lamps instead of answering the call. The Bible never said that they needed the light to meet the bridegroom.

When you are presented with an opportunity that's aligned with your purpose; it's time to make that move, it's time to make it happen, it's time to seal the deal, it's time to move forward, you cannot take that time to focus on what's missing.

What you think might be missing to get to where you want to go will send you in the opposite direction. I know people who spend more time preparing to do something than actually doing it. Stay on track. Do not turn around to fix an issue.

The Kingdom is like Three Men with Talents
(Matthew 25:14-30)...

Make a decision.

Nothing moves forward or grows without a decision being made. As in point 4 and 5, people spend so much time making decisions on handling what they think is wrong or what needs to be "taken care of", that a decision to move forward is never made. Problem solving is not decision making. Again, life is lived from the stand point of preservation instead of moving forward. I will tell a Christian in a blink of an eye, "You don't have a problem that needs to be solved, so stop wasting your Christian "walk" trying to get to where you already are".

So this leaves most people burying what they have been given in order to preserve it, so it never has the opportunity to expand into more. People get this mindset of irresponsibility because they think everything is up to God or the devil, and they sit around like dummies waiting on God to move. How stupid. God said, "In Him, we move and have our being", but most are sitting around waiting on "the move of God". All the while their talent is left buried.

Make a choice. Act. It is only then that the power of the Kingdom is active.

Many wait for the right conditions or for things to get right before they make a move or make a decision. This is why it is said, "Seek ye first the Kingdom of Heaven and His Righteousness...". In God, things are always right, so the time that is right is always right now.

Being stuck is horrible, but you're never stuck because of conditions, you can only be stuck when a decision can't be made.

The Kingdom is like a Mustard Seed
(Matthew13:31-32)...

Start the process, size doesn't matter.

Most people wait for the right conditions to make a decision to move forward. Don't do it. Decisions plus action carry great power. You must realize that momentum becomes an ally when you decide to move forward and take action. When active decisions take place it creates an energy that becomes the backbone of growth.

When you wait for the right conditions to make a move, it means you do not recognize the power that is contained within the seed of your actions. A mustard seed when planted has two properties that fly in the face of logic. First, the mustard is a very tiny seed. If you based your expectation of what a mustard tree would be based on the size of the seed, you might not ever plant the seed. The size of the seed is not representative of the size if the tree when it is fully grown. Never measure your end results based on the size of what you have to start with. Just start.

Secondly, once a mustard seed is planted, it does a superior job at growing past obstacles. Even if concrete is poured and set over the ground, generally a mustard tree will break through. This is what I mean by momentum. When you actively decide to start, you set in motion forces that can become unstoppable. So your momentum breaks through your conditions. So you handle your conditions by getting started.

The Kingdom is like a Farmer Sowing Seed
(Matthew 13:18-23)...

Cultivate your surroundings and anything you do will unfold.

Understanding is the key to life. Understanding is the key to producing what you want in life. Let me tell you a fact about information. The information for everything you can ever want or need is always there and available. It is always coming to you. What separates people who get this information and people who don't is their level of understanding. Information is never a problem when it comes to successful living, but connecting to that information can be an issue.

Here's a key that will help move you to the next level and possibly save you thousands of dollars. Yes, People pay thousands of dollars to gain information in order to be successful. It could be a simple audio program or it could be something as extensive as a seminar costing thousands of dollars, or even a full education on a particular subject. When success is not achieved then one might spend even more money trying to discover the secrets to life and success.

Here's the true secret. It is never the information that you need that's at issue, it's your surroundings. Your surroundings affect your understanding. I cannot emphasize enough, the information to gain the highest heights is always there. Most likely, you don't need to research sources of information to gain a greater life, much less pay for it. Information is always present!

Let me put it this way. I have seen people spend tens of thousands of dollars on gaining information on a particular path for success and never achieve success, and then I have seen people with very little resources become the wealthiest people in every way in their field of endeavor. What's the difference? Understanding.

What affects your understanding? It is your surroundings. Cultivate your surroundings for growth and the information that is continuously streaming towards you will become clear, and growth can then take place. You have to set your surrounding for growth. Here are the 3 negative surroundings that can't facilitate the reception of information needed for optimal growth and will rob you of understanding:

1. **Exposed existences.**

This is when you do not care enough about your goals to mind who you exchange with and where you do business. There is no focus on the land and the environment in which you make exchanges.

2. **Shallow existences.**

The only thing that is deeply rooted enough to provide optimum growth is doing what you love to do. Any other effort will be shallow and not last.

3. **Distracted existences.**

These are the things and the people that keep you busy that have nothing to do with where you are going and what you are trying to achieve.

The Kingdom is like Leaven
(Matthew 13:33)...

Decide your recipe. You are influential whether you like it or not.

Pay attention to your continual presentation. What comes from you is the leaven of life. Life does not happen to you, Life happens from you. A lot of times people blame their problems on external circumstances, but problems should be blamed on existential circumstances. If you want to change your environment, change yourself.

Many do not realize that there was a point in human history and development when the environment stopped being the influence to man's development and man became the influence for environmental development. You have to ask the question; am I primitive in how I view life? It is immature to believe that life has given you an unfair shake. Life extends from who you decide to be, and when you experience consistent conditions that you do not favor, you are witnessing a state of your own inner being.

This really makes it easy to change your circumstances, because you no longer have to focus on what needs to be fixed outside of yourself. Life's recipe extends from you. Just stick to personal development and life will follow suite. Take measurement of the state of people, places, and things around you, and you would be taking measurement of yourself. You are the little leaven that affects the whole loaf.

The Kingdom is a King who takes Account
(Matthew 18:21-35)...

Let it go. You have a Kingdom to run.

There is a scripture that parallels this one in **Matthew 6**. It states, forgive us of our debts as we forgive our debtors. Why is this important? Where is the value of letting things go?. Most people see **Matthew 6** as forgiveness of wrong doing, but both **Matthew 18** and **Matthew 6** are talking about forgiveness of financial debt.

In the Old Testament of the Bible it was common that every seventh year all debts were cancelled and forgiven or let go of. Why does a financial matter show up in a prayer taught to the disciples?

Well the clue is found in the study that we are doing now. It's a matter of the Kingdom. A couple of versus earlier in **Matthew 6,** it states, "Thy Kingdom come, Thy will be done on earth, as it is in Heaven". Now you must remember at this point that Heaven starts from within you and Heaven influences the Earth and not vice versa.

First, this goes back to the concept where the leaven affects the whole loaf. It's about the state that you are in that affects your surroundings. Secondly, it also reverts back to the concept of your understanding. What is the Word that develops in your mind? You influence your surroundings and you cultivate your surroundings; therefore your chief desire is for others to be on the level that you are. Here you not letting go as it might benefit just you, but you are letting go so that your surroundings including the people that are indebted to you are benefited. Anyone indebted to you is placed in the position of servitude as they owe you a debt. Forgiveness of the debt releases that person from that position and brings him or her to an equal position with you.

Your understanding should lead you to the very fact that God has done the same for you. God does not see you as less than He is, and He proves it by making sure that you are in no way subservient to Him, so any debt that is owed is always forgiven. So forgiveness is how we see others and how we see others is always based on how we value our own selves.

The Kingdom is like Casting a Net
(Matthew 13:47-50)...

**Go for every opportunity related to what you want.
Picking out the fish will keep you from fishing.**

Aggressiveness is key here, but it is aggressiveness without losing focus. When a net is used to fish, you plan to catch everything you can, and once the fishing is done, you only pick out what you need. Time used being selective while you are fishing will cause loss. It is the same when it is said in the earlier parable to let the wheat and the weeds grow together. In the end, the separation is done.

Now I want to remind you here, that this end does not refer to the end of earth's time, therefore making it a reference God separating the good people from the bad people, or the "saved" from "the unsaved", wherein the unsaved is cast into the everlasting fire called hell.

No, all Kingdom parables are a reference to you and are strategies for your personal growth. So the "end" here represents a local momentary end to whatever you have started. Herein lies one of the best strategies to reaching a great end. Do not spend time during the process of any type of development to use your mental energy evaluating good and bad, but maintain your focus on the task of engaging anything related to what you are doing. It's like casting a net versus a single line.

The Kingdom is like a Treasure in a Field
(Matthew 13:44)...

Know how to buy the field.

Knowing how to buy the field is about decision making. All decision making here is based off of a special knowledge. That knowledge is the knowledge of what is contained in the field. Have you ever run across a crazy bargain? It's as if the purchase you are making was just the same as robbing the store? You were so excited it made you take the money out of your wallet or purse faster?

There was no question in the decision. Buying the field is about eliminating the question from the decision. When you know the value of what you are going after, the value of everything you have has to be turned towards that effort. This is why it is important to value what is on your mind. Buying the field is about value. Many people move on their dreams without being prepared to buy the field.

The question is asked again. How bad do you want it? Before you start anything, look for the treasure. Only when you find the treasure do you make a decision. Then the decision will automatically involve taking the massive action needed for accomplishment.

When there is weak action, maybe there is no treasure or knowledge of a treasure. This also helps to determine what type of decisions to make. Many of us spend so much time chasing things that carry no value. Look for the treasure first. Hide it. Then give up all you got and buy that field.

And the Gift of God Is…

Now let's conclude the whole matter. You have to allow your imagination to work for you verses allowing your limitations to work for you. Your imagination will allow you to peer into God's gift. The Spirit provides a constant flow of information that allows for the greatest life that you can ever imagine.

Remember the wages of sin is death, but…

The only thing that has a wage, which denotes something that is earned, is sin, and sin by definition is missing the mark. What mark? And why is death the wage?

There are only two results when it comes to labor:

Nothing   &   Rest

Jesus says, come unto me all you that labor and I will give you rest. But, there are also some who labor in vain and end up with nothing. The Bible says in **Psalms 127:1**, Except the Lord builds a house, they that labor, labors in vain.

So let's start with the house. In my Father's House are many mansions. Jesus said in **John 14**, I go to prepare a place for you.

So you see here, the work of house building is done by Christ. In 1st Corinthians it states in chapter 15, Let us be steadfast and unmovable, always abounding in the work of the Lord… not our own work.

So let me be clear; there is your work and then there is the work of Christ. The wages of missing the mark, which is at any endpoint while reaching nothing, is death; but the gift of God is eternal life. The word "eternal" stems from the Greek words aei or ain, which means to be done again perpetually. The phrase "end of the world" uses the exact same words. Therefore, there is no point that you can get to, or end point that you can reach that God has not prepared a place for you. It states in Psalms 138, that even though I make my bed in hell, thou art there. So where can I go from thy Spirit?

Just like in 1st Corinthians, death is insignificant because of the gift of God. But you have to decide into the life that is eternally provided which extends beyond any type of death. **Ecclesiastes 5:18, 19** says, that it is good for a man to eat and to drink and to enjoy his labor under the sun all the days of his life which God hath given him, for it is his portion. Every man also to whom God hath given riches and wealth and hath given him power to eat thereof, and to take his portion, and to rejoice in his labor; this is the gift of God.

What does this mean? With such provisions set, it is only ours to miss only to end up with nothing or end up with what we don't want. Missing earns you the state of death, but there is still and will always be a gift beyond death. The work of the Spirit never ends because the gift is never ending.

Expected Ends

Everything you do has an end. You start a meal and then your meal comes to an end. You start school, you end school. You begin a trip, you end a trip. You start a job, you end a job. Your days have beginnings and your days have an end. You call someone on the phone and at some point the conversation comes to an end. When you fly out on an airline, your flight has an end, a termination, a terminal.

All of your "ends" have been predetermined and you are set for success by His Word that measures and counts out your success beyond your ends. **Jeremiah 29:11** says that God's thoughts are on you and they are thoughts of peace and not of evil, to give you an expected end.

God's thoughts always extends beyond evil. Where are your thoughts? Remember, it is only through our thoughts that value is assessed.

The word "end" in the Bible comes from the Greek word "telo" where we get our word "teller" as in bank teller. It also has as an extended connotation involving the word "custom". So ask yourself, what is your custom at your end -points?

Let me ask you that again…What is your custom at your end-points? The reason why the Greek word has an extended notion of "custom" denotes that at every "end" there is a "telo", "teller", or an accounting of the end. This is why I stated earlier that the concept of the judgment is not an end-of-the-world concept, but at your every "end" there should be a judgment or an accounting. With this you will either find yourself in line with the optimal thoughts that has been created, or you will find yourself in a "hollow" place.

You need to take into account at your ends whether you are dead or whether you are living in God's gift. It does not take a rocket scientist to figure this out. Here's the point:

What if you drove through the drive thru at McDonald's and ordered a full meal and then you paid full price at the 1st window, but when you got to the 2nd window they only handed you a small fry? Then you drove around again, placed the same order, paid the full price, pulled up to the window and they gave you a small fry again? Then you drove around again, placed the same order, paid the full price, pulled up to the window and they gave you a small fry again? Then you drove around again, placed the same order, paid the full price, pulled up to the window and they gave you a small fry again? How many times would you do it?

You wouldn't stand for it!!!

But a lot of times, this is done in life. We stay in the same relationships, make the same choices, go to the same dead church, experience the same situations again and again, day after day, week after week, month after month, and year after year with no accounting. At the accounting which is at every end, if it is not right, you then have a decision to make. Most people do not make decisions; they just drive around again and again, living out the same pattern.

The point is, is that you have to decide out of where you are into your portion which is God's gift. His gift should intersect with your end.

This is where you have to be a "teller" and take an account of where you are. This is why there are ends. End points are there for assessment.

Let me be clear here:

Your portion is unfolded from your thoughts. Yes. That is an exacting truth and not a relative truth. When you say or think, "I want"...there is.

Stop!

This is not magic in the sense of how most people currently understand it. At the creation of every thought...there is. "There is" sets itself up as your portion, which then unfolds into reality or into what can be experienced. Missing your "there is" is sin. What we traditionally and religiously know and understand as "sin"; drinking, smoking, adultery, fornication, lying, cheating, stealing, backbiting, etc. is not "sin", but these behaviors are a result of sin. Sin is missing your "there is", which is your portion.

Your portion is set when you think about it. Many people "think" their dreams, but many people cannot decide into their dreams, because every thought has competition. This is the gross evil stated in Ecclesiastes chapters 3 and 5.

It's simple. Options. Yes. Options to your highest life, most accurate move, your best connection, and optimal direction is the great evil. When you take your eye off your own great prize to consider another option, your portion is then missed. You then live in a hollow place or darkness until you see the light of what you want again.

Decision Strategies

Many do not end up with their desires because they can't fully decide into what's new and what's next. So here, I am giving you the 9 stages of decision-making that should be involved in every decision that you make. But I want to clue you in; these 9 stages are synonymous with the 9 stages of development that leads to the 10th part of existence, which is you. Most cannot decide into right ends so the 9 will help.

Here are the stages:

1. **Decide past distractions.**
2. **Decide past what's dying.**
3. **Decide out of what's old into what's new.**
4. **Decide in agreement.**
5. **Decide through action.**
6. **Decide in presentation.**
7. **Decide in continuance of time.**
8. **Decide up and across.**
9. **Decide towards yourself.**

Then you reach yourself. **10...**

First, you must know that when you are considering a decision, "YOU" have to be the endpoint... This is 10. You are the image of what you want to accomplish. This is why I don't believe in goal setting. Most people don't reach their goals because money is set as the end image, a place or a destination is set as an end image, that dream date or person that you desire to be with is set as an end image; a basketball star, a movie star, an idol is set as the image of the endpoint.

You must to set yourself as the chief value, and then everything else becomes a resulting reflection of you. Since every decision leads back to you, but a "you" in a different formation, you then must be careful and thorough in your decision making process.

All decisions are made based on your level of consciousness. So here it is:

Decide Past Distractions

First you must decide past distractions. Here you have to have a consciousness of multiple options. When you decide towards a specific achievement, along with the thoughts of achievement you will get corresponding thoughts of other decisions to make which can include thoughts of doubt which will lead to a decision to not start. You can also be interrupted with thoughts of other things that "need" to be done. Your attention can be called out to "emergencies" etc.

You have to have in your mind and body to move past these distractions even before they introduce themselves.

Decide Past What's Dying

Here you have to be conscious of what's not working. The first thing you must do here is notice anything around you, your house, or the place where you work; if it is broken, not working, been sitting for a great period of time, get rid of it! You must first practice not having dead or dying things around you. Next, friends, relatives and other people who are psychologically slower than you are and refuse to pick up the space, eliminate your time with them. Relationships that are slow and dying, you must kill them. All of these things play a subliminal roll in your decisions. With dead things, your decisions will die alongside. If something is not working including non-optimal relatioships, put it to rest and focus on what you have chosen to do.

Decide Into What's New

This goes back to our McDonald's drive-thru scenario. You have to break out of old patterns, especially when you keep coming up short. Here you have to have a consciousness of your place and then what's next beyond your current place. Do not be afraid of "Next". "Next" is your best friend. "Next" is the source of life. If there are "ends", then there is a "Next" after the "ends". But next cannot be achieved when you hang on to what's old. In this case, death is your friend also.

There are some things and processes you have to put to death.

Decide In Agreement

Here you must have a consciousness of right relationships. Remember, every desire that you have exist in its entirety. It might be just that the components of your desire are in other places. The only way to facilitate those components being in place for your experience is through right relationships. Here, you have to count on your ability to connect. You must practice on every level of relationship and having people around you that agree with you.

Don't let your dreams die at the next person. Every exchange that you make must be profitable. Every relationship is energy and all energy is working energy.

Decide Through Action

You must be conscious of your personal behavior. Motion is the key to memory. You must establish in your mind your dream so much to the point wherein it becomes a memory. Memory is not set in without motion. You always have to act.

You can practice your accomplishment at all times, even to the smallest degree. There is always something you can do towards what you want to accomplish.

Decide In Presentation

Here you must be conscious of your personal influence and create lines of intelligence. Remember you are the initial image of what you want to accomplish. So everything about you must say who you are and what you are doing; your behavior pattern, your office walls, your journals, your PC Tablet or Ipad, your clothes, your personal look etc.

With this, you create what I call "Lines of Intelligence", meaning the more you be who you want to be, your environment begins to coincide. People must then coincide with your presentation also. When they don't, they break your line of intelligence and that's the point where energy is drained. So to keep things flowing, make sure you put out the right presentation so that people can make the right agreements with you and towards you.

Decide In Continuance of Time

Here you have to have a consciousness of exponential completions. What this means is that at every stage of completion or completing something, you have to take measurement. In this measurement you have to be able to note some type of growth. If the growth is not there, then during the next cycle or time period, you have to do something different.

These cycles, time periods, ages, or eons can be measured in minutes, hours, days, weeks, months, years etc., but you must have stop-points, or check-points. Check your levels and your cycles.

Decide Up and Across

This is the consciousness of direction, para-events, and supply. Simply, when you decide, always decide up from where you currently are. Next, have all other points of decisions in your life to match the intensity of your main focus. I call these para-events. For example, if you are looking to make more money, decide along with that to have better health and maybe even better friends. If you are looking to have better health, decide along with that to have a cleaner house, change jobs, buy a new car, and again maybe even meet new people. If you want a better relationship, along with that, move to a new area of town, go to a new church, by some new clothes etc.

If you make a decision to advance one part of your life, but leave the rest the same, what's been left the same can pull at and destroy what you are trying to change. This is what I mean by deciding across. You will be surprised at the supply that is available to facilitate multiple decisions that is in need to be made simultaneously.

Decide Towards You

Here you must carry a continuous consciousness of your higher self. Most people are easily distracted, not because of the value that they put on what they are trying to accomplish, it is because of the value that they do not put on themselves. This is because there is a non-recognition of the higher self. So when something else makes a presentation, they move towards another perceived value in which they might feel is more important.

Put yourself first. A lot of people think that is a selfish notion. But the Bible says, Seek ye first the Kingdom of God and His righteousness and ALL these things will be added. Nothing is added to you without "You". Kindness is not noble when it comes at the expense of you being ok. It's like the airlines that tell you when there is a drop in cabin pressure and the oxygen is short, put your mask on first! A dead person can't help anybody.

These are the 9 decisions that have to be made for every one decision you make. You will then reach you. Reaching you is reaching your Spirit.

Made in the USA
Lexington, KY
13 February 2016